The Life

of

Boo Baker

The Life

of

Boo Baker

Written by Joe T Baker III

Edited by Kingdom Lyrics

First edition 2019

ISBN 978-1-7923-1360-8

Some names and identifying details have been changed to protect the
privacy of individuals

Printed in the United States of America

A & R Printing Company

1217 Claylick Rd.

White Bluff Tn 37187

Therefore, if anyone *is* in Christ, *he is* a new creation; old things have passed away; behold, all things have become new.

2 Corinthians 5:17 NKJV

Table of Contents

Acknowledgements

I want to thank God for His grace, patience, mercy and love.

I also want to thank my mother and father for their strength. I wouldn't have the strength I have had it not been for them being as strong as they are.

I want to thank my sister Brittany Burr for being a listening ear, understanding and supporting my vision

I want to thank Jessica Darden for believing in me and being there for me no matter what.

Wayne Jones, for being a listening ear and for telling me the truth whenever I needed it.

Angelique Singletary, for being the best friend I could ever ask for, and for encouraging me every step of the way.

Clifton Brown, for being like a brother from another mother, and teaching me the Word; I learn so much from you.

Christopher Williams, for showing me how to live for Christ and how to love people to Christ. I couldn't have gotten the understanding I have without you.

Chapter 1: The Beginning

My name is Joe Thomas Baker III. I was born in Clarksville, Tennessee, but raised in Springfield, Tennessee in a little blue house on Short 19th. My nickname for as long as I can remember has been Boo. My granny used to call my mom that name, and it just got passed down to me. As a young child, I had what I would consider a normal childhood. I had two siblings, an older brother by three years who I shared the same dad with, and a younger sister by five years, my mom, and my mom's boyfriend who played the father role in my life because my dad was incarcerated. My dad had two life sentences in prison for robbery and murder. However, I did get to go see my dad and visit him in prison with my younger brother. Growing up, we had material things; you name it, we had it. The new Jordan shoes came out, we had it. Go karts, we had it. Nice clothes, we had it. Nice house, we had it. This was the functioning part.

The dysfunctional part was what I didn't know at that age. My mom was dating one of the

1

biggest drug dealers in Springfield at that time. I can remember walking in the kitchen one day, opening the pantry to get some snacks, and seeing so many bags of some type of drug. I had no idea what it was at the time. I grabbed my snack and closed the pantry, but it stuck in my memory. Living in that house, I witnessed a lot of abuse. My mom and her boyfriend fought like cats and dogs almost every day. It was so frequent and so often it seemed like it was happening all the time. I mean big fights, not little fights. I'm talking about black eyes, busted noses, holes in walls, breaking dishes, screaming, hollering, fussing, a lot of verbal abuse, a lot of cussing... *a lot!*

I can remember one night when there was a big fight, I'm not sure what it was about, but I heard my mom saying, "If you're going to kill me, go ahead and kill me!" My brother and I were in our room with the door closed, crying. My mom came in crying with her hair messed up, and her face and neck scratched. She sat down with us, and I was on the left and my brother was on the right. She told us how much she loved us, and if anything happened to her, she was going to be alright... that we would be alright. She went on and on telling us how much she loved us.

She told us, "He said he's going to kill me."

As she's saying this, we could hear him in the next room hollering about how he was going to kill her. Finally, the door opened, and my mom, my brother, and I were sitting on the end of the bed crying.

My mom said, "So you're going to kill me in front of my kids?"

He had his hand behind his back, and I thought he had a gun. When he raised his hand from behind his back, it was my mom's car keys in his hand.

He pitched her the keys and said, "If you want to leave, you go ahead and leave."

We grabbed a little of whatever we could, jumped in the car, and drove to my granny's house in Clarksville, Tennessee. This was the only time I can ever remember my mom hugging me or telling me she loved me. She was never affectionate. At that age

3

it didn't bother me because I didn't know what I was missing. You don't miss what you never had. In the same way, God was never talked about in my home, *ever.* We went to church here and there, but my only understanding of God was that He died for my sins or wrong doings. I didn't know God or His word or my need of Him. What I knew was the reality of everything that was going on around me, including moving to Clarksville.

This was the beginning.

Chapter 2: Short 19th

We got to Clarksville to my granny's house. Living there was my brother, my mom, my granny, my uncle, and myself. I was still going to school in Springfield, so we got up every morning, and drove thirty to forty-five minutes from Clarksville back to Springfield. My mom would drop me off at my cousin Peanut's house to get on the bus from there. When we got out of school, we rode the bus back to Peanut's house, and then drove back to Clarksville. We did this routine every day for two to three weeks.

Living at my granny's I learned how to shoot dice. One day my uncles were shooting dice outside, and they let me shake the dice and explained the points: seven wins, eleven wins, snake eyes lose, twelve loses. They taught me the game, hands on. During the game, one of my cousins beat me and took my five dollars. When he took it, I got mad and tried to make him give it back, but he pushed me in my head and told me to leave him alone. He wouldn't give me my money back, so I went in the house and told my mom.

My mom told me, "Go outside and when he's not paying attention, kick him in the nuts."

So, that's what I did. I went back outside, and as he was standing there shaking the dice, I stood behind him and I kicked him as hard as I could in his testicles and ran back in the house. A couple days afterwards, my brother and I were playing Mortal Kombat on the game console, and our neighbor was over playing with us. My neighbor beat me in the game and was talking crazy to me, so I punched him in his mouth and busted his lip. When my mom and granny got home, he told them I punched him in his lip, and my mom made me apologize. That was the end of it, but not of my habit of being a sore loser.

My brother and I were playing in this field, and there was a lot of dry grass. We were playing with a lighter and lit a piece of the grass on fire. The whole field just went up in flames within fifteen to twenty seconds, so we took off running and hid in the woods. We waited in the woods for two hours waiting for the police and firetrucks to leave. When we finally walked in the house, my granny, my mom, and my uncle were all sitting in the living room waiting for us. There was a pack of cigarettes laying on the table.

My mom told us, "Sit down!" We sat down and she said, "So, ya'll think ya'll know how to smoke cigarettes huh?"

We told her we weren't smoking, but she thought we caught the field on fire with my granny's cigarettes. She pulled out a cigarette, lit it, and handed it to me.

She said, "Since you think you know how to smoke cigarettes, smoke it."

So, I took the cigarette, took a puff, and before I could even exhale all the smoke, she told me to take another puff. She kept repeating, "take another puff," until I smoked the whole cigarette. I probably smoked it in about thirty seconds. I was ready to throw up. When I got finished smoking, she told me to get in the shower and go to bed. That's probably the reason I was never a smoker after that experience.

Shortly after, my mom ended up taking her boyfriend back. We packed our stuff up and moved back to Springfield. I remember feeling some type of way in the car on the way back. I didn't know why I was feeling the way I felt, but I did, and my mom's boyfriend noticed because he asked me what was wrong. I just told him I felt as if something was going to happen. He tried to comfort me by promising me that he wouldn't let anything happen to us or to my mom. A couple of days after, I got off the bus and walked home. When I got there the door was cracked open, and when I walked in the house, *everything* was broken. I walked through the kitchen and all the glass dished were broken. Somebody put something in the microwave and blew it up. When I walked in the living room, all the home interior was crashed in the floor, the couches were gone, and they took a lot of stuff. I was so scared that I just walked back out and went to go play outside with the other kids without telling anybody. I played until my mom got home because I was scared to go in the house. When my mom and her boyfriend got home, he told us not to worry about it, and swept it under the rug. I still until this day don't know what happened. We ended up getting all new furniture and home interior and just went on with business as usual.

Every day after that, when I got off the bus, I would never go in the house. I would always wait until my brother got off the bus, or I'd go play until my mom got home because I was scared to go in the house alone. One day, I was supposed to be a car rider, but my uncle forgot to pick me up, so one of my teachers had to give me a ride home. When we got to the house, she told me she was going to stay in the driveway until someone answered the door. I knew no one was home, but the door was left unlocked for me, so I knocked on the door and yelled to my teacher, "They said they're coming, you can leave!" She took my word for it. When she turned around to back out the driveway, I took off running to the side of the house until she was gone. When she left, I just went to play with my friends because I refused to go in that house.

When winter came, I caught the chicken pox. I had to go to the hospital, and I stayed there over a month. At one point my heart stopped beating and they had to resuscitate me. The chicken pox was so bad, they were inside my body. I was so sick that I couldn't stand up and walk. Anytime I got out the bed and tried to stand up, I'd pass out from being too dizzy. I finally ended up being discharged and going home, but I still couldn't get up and walk. My little sister was a baby at the time, so I was only five years old. When I finally got enough strength to stand up a little, they let me hold her for the first time. While I was holding her, after about five seconds, I got dizzy, passed out, and dropped her. The next day I had an appointment, and my mom took me back to the hospital to get checked, but she couldn't find a parking spot.

She pulled off and said, "Fuck that shit, I'm going back home."

She drove me back home sick and left it at that. I always wondered why she just didn't take me in there. I don't know if it's because she was tired of the whole process or what, but I could've died. I may not have known what affection was from my mom, but after that I knew what it wasn't.

When I got better, whenever my mom changed my sister's diaper, she told me or my brother to take the diaper, tie it up in a plastic bag, and go throw it away in the trash can outside. Whenever I didn't feel like walking all the way to the trash can, I'd stand on the porch and sling it on top of the neighbor's roof. There were at least fifteen diapers on their roof, and it eventually started attracting cats. When the neighbor went to find out why the cats were on her roof, she discovered all the diapers, and came and told my mom.

My mom called for me, "Boo get your black ass in here!"

She made me find a way to climb on top of the neighbor's roof and throw all the diapers down and throw them in the trash can.

As I got a little older, around eight years old, I started taking an interest in girls. I had a cousin named Kresha who was my brother's age. She lived up the street, and I had a crush on her. She used to come down the street and play with us all the time, but Kresha and I used to dry hump a lot. We got close to messing around one time, we both had our clothes off, but we didn't do anything because she got up and left. I think we both got scared when we saw each other's bare body parts. I told my brother and one of his friends about it and then they wanted to do it too. We invited her to the house one day, and my brother and his friend went in the room and did who knows what. When they came out, I thought it was my turn, but she wouldn't let me.

I got upset so she asked me, "Well, what you wanna do? I'll let you do anything you wanna do."

I came up with the crazy idea of pouring salt down the crack of her butt, and we all laughed. I don't know how I came up with that idea.

Another cousin who was older, babysat me and my brother one day. My cousin and I were in the room, and my brother came in to ask if he could fix some cereal. She said yes, and when he walked out, she got up to close the door, and then laid down in front of the door so the door couldn't be opened. When she laid down, she pulled her pants down to her ankles, and she called me over to the door. I didn't understand or know what was going on. So, when I walked over to the door, she pulled my pants down and started "jacking me off" or using her hand to stimulate my penis to get an erection. When my penis got hard, she stood me in front of her, pulled me down, stuck my penis inside her, and moved my hips to pull me in and out of her. I was so confused, and I didn't say anything. My brother came and knocked on the door, and she told him to hold on until she finished. When she was done, she pulled up her pants, pulled my pants up, and went on about the day as if nothing happened. Being molested by my older cousin is the worst memory I have in that house.

After that I started masturbating, doing to myself what she did to me. My brother caught me masturbating once, behind the couch in the living room. When he saw me, he got scared and took off running. When he finally came back in the room, he asked me what I was doing. We weren't even teenagers yet so as a child, in my head, I was just doing what my cousin did to me. Every time I saw her after that, I tried to get her to do it again. If she was in the bed, I'd get in the bed with her and roll on top of her because even though it scared me, it felt good. She never pushed me away or rejected me, but she never did anything else to me.

Outside of girls, I was always into something. In the summertime, one of my cousins, Dee would come and hang with us all the time. This cousin was a real thief at a young age. We would go to the store and he'd steal anything he could get his hands on, and he was slick with it. One time we were leaving the store and he had some gum and a pack of Starburst.

He said, "Watch this."

He started swinging his hands really fast so the clerk at the cash register couldn't see what he had in his hands, and he made it out the store with it. We started stealing lighters for some reason, and he would steal his mom's cigarettes. We would go to this abandoned trailer, and he would always be smoking cigarettes in there. One day he asked me if I wanted to smoke one. I took one puff of that cigarette and remembered what happened with my mom, and I told him, "I do not want to smoke this, I don't even know why you're smoking cigarettes." That was the last time a cigarette touched my lips.

In the neighborhood there was a lady that lived up the street and we always referred to her as "the lady with the dogs." She had two little bitty dogs, and it didn't matter who was walking down the street, they were going to chase you. There was an old abandoned house and my brother and I would throw rocks and bust the windows out. One day when we were throwing rocks trying to break the windows, the lady let the dogs out. Those dogs chased us all around the neighborhood. We jumped on cars trying to get away from those dogs, and finally we just ran to the house and ran inside. The dogs just sat outside our house. I don't know if the dogs were trained or what, but the lady found out where we lived because the dogs stayed outside... just sitting there. Those dogs were the police. When my mom got home, the lady told my mom we were throwing rocks at the abandoned house busting the windows out, and we got a whooping for it.

Back at home, I could tell the dynamic between my mom and her boyfriend was different. The arguments were different because she wouldn't respond the way she used to, and there weren't as many fights as there used to be. In retrospect, I can say at that moment, my mom was fed up. One of my brother's friends told us that he was seeing our mom's boyfriend come through his back door at night. Another friend up the street told us the same thing. One night we heard my mom and her boyfriend arguing, and I'm sure that's what they were arguing about. The argument carried over into the next day. My mom called the family and told them she was leaving. After she made the call, my mom and her boyfriend started fighting. This was the fight of all fights. They were breaking everything and putting holes in the wall. It was a true brawl. My family pulled up while they were still fighting. They ran in and broke it up while we were going to the car with our things.

My mom's boyfriend would come out, and they'd start fighting again. We drove up the street and he got in his car to drive ahead of us and cut us off. They got out the car and fought again. This repeatedly happened all the way from the stop sign at the end of the street, to the end of the other street. When we got to the other street, one of my older cousins was having words with him about fighting my mom. My mom's boyfriend went in his car and grabbed a crowbar. He chased my cousin up the street with the bar. I had a baseball bat in my hand, so I ran up the street to where he was chasing my cousin because I wanted to help my cousin. My cousin did a spin move to get past him and came running back down the street where all the other family was. When my cousin ran past me, he took the bat out of my hand, turned around and hit my mom's boyfriend on the top of the head. As soon as my cousin hit him, his head split open and a big knot swelled on his head like a cartoon character and he was pouring blood. My mom's boyfriend had a white shirt on, but it looked like he jumped in a pool of ketchup.

When he walked past me to get in his car, he said to me, "Why would you do that to *me*?"

He got in his car and pulled off. That was the end of that relationship.

After this fight my sister went to live with her granny, my mom's now ex-boyfriend's mom, and we went back to Clarksville, but it didn't last long. My mom took us to this trailer in the projects. We were cleaning it out and I asked my mom who was moving in there. She told us that we were, and I told her I didn't want to live there, and I'd rather go back to live with her ex-boyfriend. It was the rundown side of town opposed to where we were staying with her ex-boyfriend. We ended up moving in the trailer anyways.

Once we moved in the trailer, I was around thirteen years old, and there was a lot of skipping school going on. My mom worked first shift, so she'd go in around seven in the morning, and get off around two or three in the afternoon. This allowed me to skip a lot of school days and come home before her and check the mail. I removed the mail that came from school, answered the phone when they called and told them she wasn't there, so she never knew I was skipping. My brother was learning how to drive at this time, so whenever my granny would come down, she let him drive her car because my mom would never let him drive hers. One day my granny let him drive the car and we drove all the way to Goodlettsville. When we got there the car stopped working, and he didn't call my mom or my granny. When he finally told my mom the car stopped, my mom and granny came and got us. My mom got there and was slapping my brother in the head. My granny missed work because she didn't have a car to get to Nashville where she worked.

On the way back to the house my mom said we were going to get a whooping. I felt like my brother and I were getting whooped every other day since my mom and her ex-boyfriend broke up. My brother was tired of getting whooped, so when we got out the car, he took off running. He got down to the stop sign and my mom was yelling at him telling him to come back, and he better not be running off.

He looked at me and said, "Come on bruh."

I turned around and I looked at my mom, and she said, "You bet not run."

I looked down the street and he's telling me to come on. I started walking towards him, and my mom started coming around the car to get closer to me, so I just took off running with my brother and we ran away. We ran away for about three days and stayed over one of my cousin's house.

While I was there one day, somebody knocked on the front door. Nobody was home except me and my cousin's little sister. She went to the door and saw it was my mom. I don't know how she found us, but when she told me it was my mom, I tried to run out the back door. My mom brought my uncle with her, so as soon as I ran out the back door, he grabbed me, and they took me home. I didn't get a whooping. My mom sat me down, cried, and apologized. I guess my mom was scared because my brother and I never ran away before. When they finally found my brother and brought him home, she sat us both down and talked to us. She explained what

20

she was going through and how hard it was since her ex-boyfriend wasn't around anymore. I don't think we ever got a whooping again after that.

I kept skipping school, and once I skipped with my friend Bronce. We were chilling over my friend Flip's house. I came up with the idea to ride bikes to the mall. None of us had a bike so we had to steal bikes. We walked around the neighborhood and found three bikes to steal and rode all the way to the mall. The distance to this mall in the car was about thirty to forty-five minutes. It took us four hours to ride down to the mall. The most exciting part about the ride, was this big hill everyone called "The Ridge." That was the hill we were looking forward to on the way there. After forty-five minutes of riding the bikes we started to get discouraged about the distance because we hadn't gotten anywhere in comparison to where we were going, but we were also a good distance away from home to just turn around and go back. So, we went all the way to the mall, stopping to chill at a couple of stores along the way to steal drinks and candy.

When we finally made it to the mall, we just walked around because none of us had any money. While we were walking around, we started to see adults that we knew, so we decided to leave so no one would tell our moms. We went across the street from the mall to this Tennessee sports fan store and stole all kinds of Tennessee Titans merchandise. I'm not sure how we pulled it off, but all of us left the store with a jersey on. When we left there, we went to this Mexican restaurant. We went in and asked the employee if we could sit down, and he said yes. We sat down and started talking about the ride back home. Bronce started talking about how he didn't want to ride the bike back home, and we needed to call our mom. We looked at him like he was crazy because we already skipped school, so to be caught all the way by the mall would be even more trouble. Flip and I went to go use the bathroom. While we were in there, Bronce got on the phone and called his mom without us knowing. We came back out and told him to come on, and he told us his mom was on the way to come get us. We wanted to beat him up.

When Bronce's mom, Flip's mom, and Flip's mom's boyfriend got there, they got out the truck and Bronce and Flip immediately got a whooping from their moms. They made them pick up their bikes and put them in the back of the truck. I was just sitting there looking. My mom was still at work, but they told me my mom was going to get me too as soon as I got home, because they already called and told her. In the back of my mind I was thinking, "Man, I'm not getting a whooping cause I don't even get whooped anymore." The whole ride they were telling Flip and Bronce how they were going to get another whooping, how they were grounded, and how they were going to return the bikes to the rightful owners. All the while I'm laughing, and Bronce's mom kept reminding me that my mom was going to give me a whooping when I got home. I hadn't had a whooping longer than I could remember. When I got home, my mom came in and asked me what happened, and I told her. She slapped me upside my head a few times and called me stupid, but I didn't get a whooping. She told me I better not do it again and that was the end of it.

Later on, Flip and I went to Walmart and we stole a bunch of paintball guns. We went to empty check-out lines and put bags in our pocket. We walked around the store, found the guns, and put them in the bags like we already paid for it and walked right out with them. When we got home, we couldn't figure out how to work it, so we went back and asked the employee for instructions, and he advised us that we needed air for them to work. We did the same thing we did with the paintball guns, went and got bags, put what we needed in the bags and walked out the store with them. As soon as we got them working, Flip took three shots at my mom's trailer leaving three orange splashes. After that we went around the neighborhood shooting everyone's houses and cars. We hid the guns under Flip's trailer where the dogs were kept. Flip's stepdad went to feed the dogs one day and he saw the paintball guns. There was already a lot of talk around the neighborhood about who was shooting the neighborhood up with the paintballs. Flip told his stepdad that the other guns were mine because we had two a piece, and his stepdad told my

mom. My mom slapped me upside my head a few
times, but I didn't get a whooping.

We were only in the trailer a year before my
brother got in the streets and started selling dope with
one of his friends. He'd come in the house and give
me five dollars, but he'd have bank rolls of money. At
the time I didn't know or understand where he was
getting the money from. About four or five months
after he started selling dope, he got pulled over
somewhere, and his friend threw the dope in the
floorboard, so they both ended getting charged and
got sent to DCS custody. He did a year while I was at
home by myself. We would go see him and bring him
home every other weekend for a home pass. He'd
come home on Friday and we'd take him back on
Sunday. While my brother was gone, I started acting
out of character because I didn't have anyone, and I
started getting in more trouble. My brother was gone,
my dad wasn't around, and my sister was living with
her granny. My mom worked all the time and when
she wasn't working, she was sleep. It was my own way
of crying out for attention from the impact of being
alone.

Then my birthday came, and it was the only birthday worth remembering from my childhood. It was my fourteenth birthday. I remember this one because this was around the time, we started seeing rats in the house, and I could hear them at night running all over the place. I never had a birthday party before. My mom bought a six pack of cupcakes, put candles in them, and I blew them out. I didn't get any presents because we didn't celebrate or make a big deal about birthdays. My granny came a few days afterwards and bought me a chrome Huffy bike with the pegs on it. I'll never forget it because that was my favorite bike. I had the bike around the time school got out, and this was also the time I got in a relationship with this girl.

My friends and I would walk to the YMCA all the time in big groups, and when I got there, I would flirt with this girl until we started unofficially dating. Neither of us said it, but it was understood. When school let out, she failed seventh grade which was the grade ahead of me, but she didn't tell anyone, including her parents, and led everyone to believe she was going to summer school. Everyone who had summer school rode their bike there. She'd come and ask me if she could ride my bike to summer school, so I let her ride my bike everyday not knowing that when they'd go to school, she'd just ride my bike around town for a few hours until everyone got out of school, just to make it seem like she was really going. When school started back, I found out she was held back because she was in some of my classes and she finally told me the truth.

One day I walked in the house and saw my mom having sex on the couch with someone I didn't know. I closed the door back quickly and locked it. She still doesn't know that I saw that, but it scared me. My mom and her boyfriend had been broken up a while, and I hadn't seen him for some time. My brother and I knew something was going on because at a certain time of the day my brother and I would have to go in our room and close the door. We never got to see him or know who he was. The other telltale that something was up was this was the only time my mom would cook. Every time my mom would start cooking, we knew we'd have to go in our room shortly thereafter and close the door. It came out that

27

my mom fell in love with a married man. This is also why he couldn't be in our life. I always wondered why she chose him when he wasn't going to be available the way that we needed because he had his own family at home. It wasn't a short-term fling either because she stayed with him for years until he died. He never spoke to us, or played a role, he was just there.

Living in this trailer is when we got introduced to my grandfather because he lived up the street. Whenever he walked to the corner store which was around the corner from us, he'd come check on my mom. My grandfather was petty, and whenever he came around, he never really gave us anything aside from a couple dollars here and there. While Flip and I were at his trailer, he made me mad one time, so I intentionally took his cigarette packs and burned them up so he wouldn't have anything to smoke. One time as I was burning a cigarette, it dropped on the floor and started burning the carpet. When I saw the carpet burning, it gave me an idea and I burned the carpet with the lighter. When I burned the carpet, I didn't think it would catch fire and send everything else up in flames. So, Flip and I left while the carpet was burning to walk to Wal-Mart to steal.

By the time we got back from Wal-Mart there were fire trucks, ambulances, and police everywhere. The trailer was disintegrated. It completely burned down to the ground. Everyone was standing outside asking what happened, so I lied and blamed it on my cousins up the street. I said I saw them around the trailer, and they burned it down. The next day they got in trouble for it, so after school one day, my cousins and a gang of their friends chased me and Flip home. We ran in the house and locked the door. They banged on the door telling me they were going to get me and threw my mom's porch furniture off the porch. This went on for weeks every time they saw me walking home.

Chapter 3: Carden Circle

We moved again to Carden Circle and my brother was still locked up. I started hanging with my cousin Dee that I didn't get to hang with much because he was in and out of juvenile detention, but he was one of my favorite cousins. His mom was a big-time dope lady. We used to go over his house and he had all the video games, bikes, and latest material things. He had the life we used to have when my mom was dating her dope dealer ex-boyfriend. Dee got out of juvenile detention one time and he was living in a foster home. Foster home was one of the lowest security level places they sent people coming out of juvenile detention. He still had restrictions like a group home, and he also got weekend passes. His foster parents were well off as far as I could tell because he was always dressed nice when he came around on weekend passes. Later, he was on the run from foster care, but I didn't know. He came and told my friend Derek and I where his foster parents kept their money at during the holidays, and we planned to go get it.

We walked to this big house, and the plan was to break the window, Dee and I go inside and get the money, and Derek stand outside as a lookout. We broke the window; Dee and I went inside and ran upstairs to get the money. It was around 1500 to 1600 dollars, so we split the majority of it between ourselves, and gave Derek a little for being a lookout. A few days later, a detective came to my house. He asked for me and my mom, but my mom wasn't home. He told me he'd be back, and he showed me a picture of my cousin, Dee, giving a statement about what happened that night. I told him that I hadn't been around Dee lately. He eventually came back and spoke with my mom. She took me down to the police station, and I ended up getting charged.

I came up with the idea of going to speak to Dee's foster parents, whose house we broke into. They weren't there but Derek and I found out they worked at the bank, so we walked there. When we spoke with the woman, we lied and told her we went there so Dee could get the rest of his clothes, but when we got there, he came outside with all this money, and he gave us some money and we went to the mall and spent it. She believed us because Dee had a reputation for being in and out of trouble. She told us to tell the judge that. When the court date came, Dee, Derek, and I were standing before the judge. I was excited because I thought we were going to get out of it, and the only one that was going to be arrested was Dee.

The people we robbed were present, and so was my mom, and Derek's aunt. The judge asked me first what happened. I tried to sell the same story about helping my cousin with his clothes. While I'm mid-sentence in my lie, Dee cut me off and told the judge that wasn't what happened and preceded to tell him the true story. The judge immediately made the decision that Dee was telling the truth. He put Dee back in DCS custody, and he looked at Derek and told him he was giving him five days. When he told him that, I got excited because I thought my sentencing would be light like Derek's. When he looked at me, he told me he was placing me in DCS custody as well. I turned around and looked at my mom, and she gave me a careless look like, "I don't know why you're looking at me, they're going to lock your black ass up." I turned back around and realized they were serious and began bawling. They took me to the back, and I was still crying. I remember telling them they had the wrong one, over and over.

Dee hollered from the next cell, "No, they got the right one, ya'll tried to tell that lie on me!"

This was the first time that I went into DCS custody.

They moved me to a different detention center for temporary placement and there were only about three cells in the facility. I remember everything I was feeling because I was young, this was my first time away from home, I was used to going outside to play, going in the refrigerator whenever I wanted, doing whatever I wanted, but now I was in a cell. The smell was different, and the food was horrible. We could only shower on Mondays, Wednesdays, and Fridays and they only lasted less than five minutes. Derek was in the cell next door, and as long as he was there, I was okay to a certain extent. Whenever one of us woke up we would beat on the wall. I couldn't see him, and we weren't allowed to talk to each other, so throughout the day whenever we needed each other, we'd beat on the wall back and forth. We would make beats back and forth for hours and that gave me a little sense of peace.

The day came for him to leave and the officer came and told Derek he was leaving so she had to get him ready. She gave him his clothes back and I could see and hear him throw his clothes out and get his shoes back. When his aunt came to get him, he looked back at me and told me to keep my head up. I tried to act tough and told him I was okay, and told him to take care, but when he walked out the door, it was probably the worst feeling in the world. I was locked in a place with a bunch of people I didn't know, and I was homesick. I probably sat in the cell and cried for the next two days. They finally came and got me and moved me to another detention center. This detention center was a big pod with a lot of kids. The building probably held between forty to fifty kids. When I got there, I had to go through the cough and squat procedure, which is stripping down completely naked, squatting and coughing at the same time to verify nothing was being smuggled in through my anus. They took me to this pod and gave me a bed roll which was a care package with a washcloth, towel, horrible toothpaste, horrible deodorant, a blanket, pillow, and two pillowcases.

Immediately people were asking me what gang I was in and what I was affiliated with. Where I came from, gangs weren't a thing, and all the gang and affiliation stuff was new to me. They put me in a cell with someone who was probably about a year or two older than me who was there for robbery. I walked in the cell and I was trying not to cry, but he knew I was upset. He asked me if I had been locked up before and I told him I hadn't. He told me it was his second time being locked up, but he seemed cool like he was just chilling. He told me I would be alright, and he told me how I needed to carry myself, and what all was going on in the unit. I realized that I had to adapt quickly and make the adjustments because if not, they'd sense my fear, I'd be run over. When we had open pod, which was recreational time, people were playing spades, dominos, chess, and games alike. I didn't know how to play any of the games because we didn't play them back at home. I learned how to play everything but chess.

I was only there for about a week before they transferred me somewhere else. They took me to a temporary placement at a group home. There were ten kids there, six in one room, and four in another. It was better than the detention center because we got home cooked meals, we could use the phone, we got to take real showers, we got to go on outings, and we had a basketball team that would play against other group homes. After I was there for a month, they finally gave me a home pass for forty-eight hours. I spent the entire time with my girlfriend, and went out to eat, and had as much fun as I could. After my home pass I was moved to my permanent placement where I would stay for the remainder of the time. My permanent placement was a larger group home. When I got there, they still questioned me about my gang affiliation. By this time, I was more informed about what gangs were and what they meant by affiliation. There was this one guy who explained to me that he was GD, which is a set or group called Gangsta Disciple within the Folk gang, and he was showing me the hand signs. That triggered a flashback in my memory of my dad having a pitchfork burned into his index finger and his thumb. I remember asking him what it was, and he told me he was a Gangsta. So, as the guy explained the gang, I made the connection with my dad, and instantly I knew that's what I wanted to be.

After another month, I was granted home passes again. I got to go home every weekend for forty-eight hours, and I always spent it the same way, with my girlfriend. The group home was a more laid-back facility than the detention centers, so it never clicked in my mind that I never wanted to get in trouble again. The punishment was tolerable. I spent five months and five days in custody. I got out July third. When I got out, I was fifteen and excited to be starting my freshman year. The first thing I did was go to my basketball coach because I wanted to hoop.

Chapter 4: High School

I got to high school and I talked to the coach, introduced myself, and mentioned who my brother was because he was well known for playing basketball. I already missed the tryouts, but I told him that I wanted to be on the team. He told me he'd give me a shot and instructed me to come to practice. After one practice he told me I could join the team. I made good grades the entire season because if you had two F's or more, you got benched or you had to run a mile. Basketball became my first love, and as long as I could play nothing else in the world mattered.

After a while my grades dropped, and I made two F's. Instead of getting benched, I told him I wanted to run the mile. He made me run the mile before one of the most important games playing an undefeated team. The mile had to be timed, and if you didn't finish the mile within fifteen to thirty minutes, you had to run the mile again. I had to run the mile while the other team was already there, and the gym was already packed. My coach was good for making us run for any reason, so while I was running, I was ahead of time because I was used to it. As people came in, other people told them why I was running and what my goal was. After a while I started getting tired, but the entire gym was rooting for me. I made the mile, but then the coach started me in the game with not time to rest. I still played the best game I ever played with twenty-five points on the board.

When the season was over, I started slacking in my grades, and I started getting in trouble again. I kept getting in school suspension, and out of school suspension. I wasn't interested in school anymore. I was so careless that I got mad over something petty I heard a classmate say about me, I walked out of class, walked into his class while his teacher was teaching and called him out on it. I approached him to fight him and they called the principle and stopped it before it could happen. I got kicked out of school for that and sent to alternative school. Flip was also in alternative school, and neither of us liked it so we made a habit of skipping. This is how I got into stealing cars.

One weekend Flip, my friend DLo and another friend and I were walking from shooting basketball at the center and it was snowing. A guy pulled up to a building and left his car running. Flip and I hopped in his car and took off. The guy came out screaming for us not to steal his car. We sped off as fast as we could in the snow, fishtailing, until we got to the end of the street and pulled over for DLo and the other friend to get in the car. We would park the car behind this hotel so we could go get the car and drive it whenever we needed it. Flip's birthday came and his mom gave us some money under the impression that my mom would be driving us to the mall to buy him some shoes. We drove ourselves to the mall in the stolen car, and I was only fifteen and he just turned sixteen. He bought his shoes and we were headed back to Springfield. We were flying down this straight road in the snow, and I lost control of the car. We spun into a ditch and banged the car up really bad. We took off running and left the car. A few days later we stole another car the same way. Someone left their car running and we hopped in and took off. We parked the car at the same hotel.

One night we were driving, and the police passed us, and noticed the car. The police U-turned and we all decided to stop and jump out the car and take off running. DLo, one of my cousins, Jeff, and I hopped out and took off running. Jeff's foot got ran over so he got held up, and the police caught him. His parents specifically were going to really be upset because they did not play. He wasn't even supposed to be out that late, but he told them he was staying the night with me. We walked all the way to his house which was a thirty-minute walk. When we got there, we knocked on the window and he told us he was ok and that he wasn't going to say anything. The next morning, he and his mom came knocking on my door. I answered, she asked for my mom and I told her that she wasn't there. My mom heard, and she came in the living room and asked what was going on. His mom immediately told her that we stole a car, and her son got caught, and they were going to charge him and lock him up. She wanted us to go down to the police station and tell them that my friends and I were with him.

I looked at my mom and told her, "I wasn't with him, I don't know why he's telling that lie."

I didn't want any parts of going back to DCS custody. They came in and sat down. They continued trying to explain, and they kept trying to get him to say what happened, but he wouldn't say anything. He shook his head in agreement that I was with him, but he wouldn't tell the story. He eventually told DLo was with us, and we went to his house. His mom said the same thing to DLo's mom, that she wanted us to go down there and take the charge together.

DLo said the same thing I said, "I wasn't with him, I don't know what he's talking about, I don't know why he's telling that lie."

I cosigned, "Me either, I don't know why he's lying on me."

DLo's stepdad came in and said, "Those two right there are sticking together."

Our moms all agreed that we all needed to go down and admit fault. They all thought we were lying because there was no reason for Jeff's mom to make it all up. We got ready to leave to go down to the police station and I took off running. They ended up going down to the station, but nothing happened. He ended up getting some community service hours, and that was the end of it. However, Flip and I were still skipping alternative school, and we ended up stealing a truck. We skipped school one time and went to this trap house. It was an abandoned house that had cable, and everything hooked up, guns all over the place, and people smoking weed. After we left there, we went to my granny's apartment in Goodlettsville. I heard my granny tell my mom that we were in a gray truck. She asked me whose truck we were in, and I told her to get off the phone. They knew at that moment; we stole the truck. I told Flip to go park the truck behind my granny's apartment. My granny took us back to Springfield, and my mom wanted us to go down to the police station, but I refused to go. However, Flip went and told them everything. They gave us a court date, and I knew I was going to get locked up because I had a truancy charge from skipping alternative school on top of stealing cars.

While I waited for my court date, I started having sex. I willingly lost my virginity to this girl who had a crush on me. I knew it because she always tried to talk to me. One day everyone kept trying to get us to mess around so they put us in the back room, and that was the first time I experienced popping someone's cherry. It scared me because there was blood everywhere. After that I started having sex all the time. Shortly after, I started dating Michelle and it was hard for me to even get a kiss from her. Around Halloween her mom was going to take us to a haunted house. When we were preparing to leave, she realized she forgot something, and walked back to her room to get it. I followed her back there. When she came out of the room, she turned the light off, I leaned in and got my first kiss. After that we kissed all the time, on the bus, in school, at home, anytime we could. I went over her house every day and spent the entire day.

We finally agreed that we'd have sex for the first time on Christmas. My granny was still working at a hotel, so she told us that she was getting my cousin, his friend, my girlfriend, and I a room. On

Christmas morning I woke up at my cousin's house and heard someone saying Candyman was killed. When I heard that, I thought to myself, "Aw man, now I'm not going to get none." Candyman was my girlfriend's dad. I felt bad for her, but at the same time I was really looking forward to having sex with her. I called around looking for her and I couldn't find her. I spoke with her sister, and her sister told me she was looking for me too. When I found her, she said she still wanted to go to the hotel with us because she wanted to be around me. My granny came and got us and took us to the hotel. We still had sex that night. I took her virginity on the same day her dad died.

After Christmas, we started having sex like rabbits everywhere and anywhere we could, and she got pregnant. When she told me, I decided to tell my mom. I walked in my mom's bedroom and she was sitting on the phone laughing and gossiping as always. She asked me what I wanted and I told her my girlfriend was pregnant.

She said, "Boy if you don't get out my room playing with me."

I told her I was serious and walked out her room. My mom didn't believe me until Michelle started getting morning sickness, and I called my mom to come get us. She came and got us on three different occasions and let us stay at home. After that my mom said she wasn't coming to get us anymore, and she was going to tell Michelle's mom. I didn't think she was actually going to do it until we got sent to the assistant principal's office and her mom was there. The assistant principal said he'd give us some privacy and walked out.

Michelle's mom asked me, "You have something you need to tell me?"

I replied, "No ma'am."

She looked at Michelle and said, "Is there something you need to be telling me?"

She didn't respond, she just looked at her mom.

Her mom asked her, "Are you pregnant?"

Michelle shook her head yes.

Her mom looked at me and asked, "So, what are you going to do? Are you going to get a job? Cause you know you're going to have to take care of this baby, cause me and your momma ain't taking care of this baby for ya'll."

I told her I would get a job and she asked me to step out so she could speak to my Michelle alone. They talked, and the cat was out the bag moving forward; we told everyone.

I was unfaithful to her even though I cared about her. We took Flip's mom's car, and we picked up one of my female classmates, Andrea, and took her to the woods and ran a train on her. We had been talking about going to Atlanta, so we told Andrea that we wanted her to go with us. She agreed, and later that night we returned Flip's mom's car, and we went to go break in one of our friend's house. One day while I was over his house playing the game console, I beat him and he got mad, went in his dad's room and got his gun, put it in my face and told me to get out his house. So, I wanted to break in his house to get that gun. We broke in and searched the house and found the 357. We went to this liquor store to wait on someone to get out of their car and leave it running, but nobody did. We gave up and decided to walk to my house.

I was wearing a RIP B White shirt. He was my friend who had recently got killed. That had a major impact on me because we just started getting close. When I found out I was leaving from getting my hair braided.

The girl who was braiding my hair yelled out, "B White just got killed!"

I yelled, "That can't be true!" I jumped in the car and got to the place he was killed, and they just transported him off, and all the blood was still in the street and everyone was standing around. I looked at one of B White's best friends and asked him whose blood it was, and he told me it was Bobby's. That broke my heart.

So, I was wearing my B White shirt as we were walking up the hill on the way to my house. Flip told me that he saw two girls get out of Dallas' truck. This truck was infamous in our town because it was burnt orange and sat on twenty-four-inch rims during the time big rims were popular. When Flip said two girls just hopped out the truck, we ran back to the side of the liquor store. One of the girls was on her way back to the car, but I had my gun out and asked her where the keys were. Before I could really ask, she told me the keys were in the truck, so we jumped in, pulled off, and drove to my granny's job. I only had about ten to fifteen dollars in my pocket, and Flip had none. I got out and told Flip to drive around until I came back out. I went in and asked my granny for some money, and she gave me about thirty dollars. When I came back out both truck doors were open, and the truck was surrounded by people.

I walked over to ask Flip what happened, and he said, "I didn't see that lil bitty ass car and I hit it."

I knew we were headed for trouble hitting a car in a stolen vehicle. I looked around in the truck and the keys were missing, but Flip said someone in the crowd had them. I walked over and asked who

49

had the keys and the valet at my granny's job said he
had them, and he was calling metro police, and they
were on the way. I lied and said the truck was a
birthday present, and I needed to know who had my
keys. He kept saying he had them, but he refused to
show them to me. I told him I wanted to make sure
he had the keys in his possession because I didn't
want anyone to jump in my truck and pull off. So, he
pulled the keys out his pocket and dangled them in
the air to prove he had the keys.

I looked at Flip to see if he was going to grab
it and he looked scared, so I knew he wasn't. I
grabbed the keys, we took off running to the truck,
and we pulled off. We took off to Atlanta after
dumping everything that was in the car like clothes,
food, and cell phones. We only kept the rap CD's and
a jar of Dro, which is high quality marijuana. We
didn't know where we were going, but we just kept
straight and ended up in Atlanta. We passed by a club
and Flip told me to put the truck in neutral so we
could show off. Everyone surrounded the truck and
was jumping on the truck, having a good time. We
left there and the sun started rising, and we were low

on gas with not enough money to get more. We sat there brainstorming trying to figure out a way to get gas. I told Flip to get the gun out the glove compartment because I had an idea.

I told him we were just going to start pulling people over by getting in front of them in the truck and taking their money, and he said okay. We saw this one guy at the grocery store dropping someone off, and when he pulled off, we followed him, cut him off, and I jumped out the truck and put the gun on him. He threw his wallet out the window and he had about fifteen dollars. When I looked at the guy and saw how scared he was, it excited me and made me want to shoot him. I told Flip I was going to shoot him. He told me not to, so after standing there for a few minutes playing around, we got in the truck and pulled off. We put that money in the gas tank. I felt like I experienced another level of power from having a gun in my hand and from the amount of fear he had.

We robbed another guy on the highway and got forty dollars before we left that side of town to be cautious about the police and went to another side of town. This side of town had a lot of big houses, so I knew we were in the right spot. We got to a four way and there was a woman driving a BMW while she was talking on the phone. She flashed her lights telling us to go. I made it seem like I was turning, but I cut her car off and Flip jumped out with the gun. She was startled, threw her phone, threw her car in reverse, and put her hands up. The car was swerving backwards because she didn't have her hands on the wheel and the car swerved into a ditch and smashed into a tree. The woman hopped out and took off.

Flip came back to the truck and said, "Man that bitch is crazy, she jumped out the car and took off running."

I asked him did she have her purse with her when she ran, and he said no. So, I told him to go back to the car and take her purse. He jumped out, took her purse, came back to the truck, and we pulled off. He went through the purse for five minutes and couldn't find anything. I unzipped the first zipper and found 1500 dollars.

We found a parking garage where we decided to park, and I went to sleep. Flip was smoking weed and listening to music, and fell asleep, so when I woke up and tried to start the truck, it was dead. I was upset so I was yelling at him and smacking him, telling him we needed to figure something out. We decided to get out and walk to find a jump. We walked downtown and went to underground mall and bought new clothes and shoes without showering or brushing our teeth. Flip needed his hair braided because he had his hair in a ponytail. One of the hair salons were charging a hundred dollars just for straight back braids.

Flip said, "I don't care how much money I have; I'm not paying that much."

A guy who overheard us saw us come out of the salon and told us his cousin could braid Flip's hair. He started walking with us, and we were all walking and talking. Flip told him we had a truck on twenty-four-inch rims, but the battery was dead, and we needed a jump. I looked at him like, "What are you doing?" The guy told us that all the cabs had jumper cables and would give you a jump if you flagged them down. We walked to the area where the parking garage was located, and the guy saw someone he knew who happened to have some jumper cables. They gave us a jump, so we gave them twenty dollars.

When the guy saw the truck we were riding in, he got excited and wanted to hang with us. We told him about the club we saw, and he told us that the club was called Envy and was a teen club. So, he showed us the ropes. He was eighteen, and we told him we were from Tennessee and he told us he could get us a hotel room if we wanted to stay. He got us a hotel room in his name, and he kept riding around with us, asking us to take him to the store, we were buying him food, and he was in control of the CD player in the truck. He was too comfortable. I looked at Flip and without speaking we agreed that this guy needed to go.

We told the guy a lie, that we were on the way to pick up my brother, and we would have to drop him off where we picked him up at, and then we'd be back to get him. He was reluctant to go, but we dropped him off, and little did he know the world of trouble he had gotten away from. We planned to go to the hotel and go to sleep, but I couldn't find it. While I'm driving around a police car gets behind me. I hit a couple of turns to verify that he was actually following me, and he was definitely following me. By the time I woke Flip up to tell him we were being followed, there were six cars behind us. Flip reached down to put his shoes on. A cop car was coming from the left and the right. We faked a turn and got a head start. Flip kept jumping up and down telling me to find an interstate. We finally found one, and an Avalanche truck was getting on the interstate at the same time as us. We sped up and turned to beat the truck. When we beat the truck, it blocked the police and gave us an additional head start. We were flying down the highway bobbing in and out of traffic. We found an exit that had a descending hill. We got off on the exit and stopped at the end of the hill. We saw about twenty police cars flying past the exit we got off at.

Flip reached in the glove compartment and got the gun and gave it to me and asked me what we were going to do. I told him I didn't know and gave the gun back to him. We pitched the gun back and forth until I finally rolled the window down and threw the gun out. He asked me again what we were going to do. I turned around to go back up the ramp towards oncoming traffic. All the cars kept dodging us, blowing their horn, and somehow, we made it out alive. As we were driving, Flip told me we needed to turn around, so I made a U-turn in the middle of the interstate and stopped all the traffic. We took off up the interstate in the opposite direction and kept straight until we passed a sign that said we were in Alabama. We found a park that had a hotel nearby, so we pulled over. We sat there for a minute and decide we'd have to take someone else's car and ditch the truck. We couldn't find anyone at the park except two girls who caught on to us and called us out. We got scared and went back to the truck.

Flip was sitting there quiet, so I asked him what was up. He broke down crying and said he wanted to go home. That made me start crying and I agreed I was ready to go home too. He asked me how we were going to get there, and I told him I didn't know. We still had money left, and I secretly kept some for myself in my sock. We drove to a gas station. There was an eighteen-wheeler there and we asked him how to get back to Nashville, Tennessee. He told us to take 65N all the way through and we'd run into it.

I told Flip he'd have to drive because I drove the entire time and I needed a break. He drove and I went in the back of the truck and went to sleep. When I woke up there were cars flying past us as Flip told me we were out of gas. We pushed the car off the road. We decided we had to do something because if the police rode by and stopped, we'd be caught. There was a ramp off to the side of us, so we thought to take some big rocks and line them up to obstruct traffic to get someone to get out and move the rocks, but that plan failed. We saw a gas station far off and decided we had to walk there. We could see ahead that it was a big rain cloud in that area, but not in the area where we were. When we got to that area, it turned out to be bugs. They had everything covered, from the light poles to Flip's ponytail.

We got to the gas station and were swatting the bugs, trying to get them off us because they were everywhere. The attendant asked us where we came from and we told him our parents ran out of gas, and they sent us to the gas station to bring some gas back. The attendant told us he didn't sell gas jugs, so he didn't know how we'd carry the gas back. We had to do something, so we bought milk jugs and carried two a piece back to the truck. We had enough gas to make it to the gas station. When we got there the attendant asked where our parents were, but we brushed him off because we just wanted to get gas and go home. We used that fill up to get back home.

We got home and decided to go to Rivergate skating rink to leave the truck there. We wiped the truck down and left it. We walked to the gas station to call a friend.

As soon as he knew it was me, he said, "Man bring that truck! Everybody knows ya'll have that truck!"

I immediately hung up on him because we were using a payphone. Flip called his girlfriend, and I

58

could tell they were arguing but I didn't know what about. I just knew he kept reassuring her that everything was okay. When he hung up, he said his girlfriend said we could come over, and she lived fifteen minutes from where we were. We walked over there and as soon as she answered the door she was cussing and going off on me.

"I know you're the one who got him into stealing cars, I'm calling Metro, you got me fucked up!"

She was yelling all kinds of accusations and obscenities. Flip tried to calm her down while I went to the restroom. I used her stuff to wash up, brushed my teeth with a toothbrush that was in there, and everything. When I came out, she was still going off. I decided to call my brother to come and get us so we could leave. When he came, he blew the horn, I stepped outside to make sure it was him, and when I got back, they set all my bags outside of the door. I started knocking on the door to get Flip to come out, but his girlfriend was continuously yelling and cussing. I went to get my brother to help me, and we tried to kick the door in, but we were unsuccessful. We were drawing attention and the neighbors started coming out. She kept yelling that she called Metro and they were on their way. The entire time Flip didn't say anything, so my brother and I decided we had to leave. He took me to his girlfriend's mom's house and let me stay there.

Flip and I still had an upcoming court date for the first truck we got caught with, and we possibly had another for this truck. I had a child on the way with Michelle, but there was another girl who said that she was pregnant by me. She was two grades ahead of me and I had a crush on her. We messed around maybe three times, but I stopped messing with her. When I stopped, one of my friends started messing with her. When I found out that he was messing with her too, I said, "Let's just run a train on her." We went over to her house, but she wouldn't let us. So, my friend and I sit and discuss how to pull it off. The plan was for me to act like I was sleep and if my friend started messing around with her, I was going to wake up, and we'd both do it. The plan was successful.

I faked sleep, she got naked, and I woke up and asked to join in on the fun. After that I brought a different friend to do the same thing. I told him once he heard us messing around, to walk in on us. I only had two condoms, so I gave one to him. While I was messing around with her the condom busted so I went to get the last condom from my friend. He gave me the condom and left because he wasn't going to be able to join in without a condom. I used that condom, and that one busted too, so we ended up having unprotected sex using the pull-out method. I didn't hear anything from her for three to four months until she called me and told me to come and see her. I walked to her house and as soon as I walked in the door she turned around and showed me she was pregnant. I told her she couldn't have the baby, and then I told her it wasn't even mine but she was convinced that I was the only one she was messing with. The only thing I was worried about was my girlfriend finding out because she was the one that I loved. I stressed to her that Michelle could not find out about it.

To top it off, we were all in the same school and I couldn't have two girls walking around pregnant by me. She said she was too far along to get an abortion, so I started mistreating her. I tried to get her to drink a bunch of alcohol to see if she would miscarry. I kicked her in her stomach, jumped on her stomach in the bed, all kinds of things, but nothing worked. Once, I took her outside, bent her over the step, and kicked her in her stomach, but that didn't work either. I resolved to making her a Pepsi and bleach cocktail. I made her drink the whole thing. She fell out on the floor and I stepped over her and walked out while she was yelling and crying. I started thinking about my dad that night wondering if he was going to go to hell for murder. I called my uncle and asked him if my dad was going to hell, but he told me he wasn't and explained forgiveness. The entire time it was really me I was worried about. I asked God to forgive me. The next day I called her and she told me it didn't work, but that she never wanted to see me again. She told me how I made her feel and how badly I was treating her all because I didn't want my girlfriend to find out. As she cried, she told me how wrong I was. She told me she wouldn't tell anyone that the baby was mine, and she'd raise it on her own.

While I'm staying with my brother's girlfriend's mom, I was going to every doctor's appointment with Michelle. When my court date came, I told my mom I wasn't going to go to court so I could see my child being born. At first my mom agreed, but then the word circulated that we stole the truck at gun point, so there was a shoot to kill out on us, and we were marked as armed and dangerous. My mom said we needed to go to the court date, so we went, ended up back in DCS custody and I missed the birth of my child. I called home every chance I could to see if she had the baby yet, and one day my mom told me she had her that morning. I couldn't cry right then because other guys were around and I didn't want to display weakness. I went in my room and cried because I was upset that I missed it. While I was calling home, word was getting out about the other baby, and the girl was telling people that the babies looked alike. I called home and my mom said she had her baby and she nicknamed the baby after me. I called her and she said the baby was mine and looked

like me, but I still denied the baby. Michelle found out
and was so upset that she broke up with me, and
moved on, all while I was in custody. I had to keep
myself together because this detention center was
worse than the others; people were getting stabbed,
and there were fights every day.

When I had my first fight, I knew I had to win
because if you lost a fight, you got picked on. We
were playing spades, and the guy I was playing lost
and started talking crazy. We started arguing, he got in
my face, and he tried to swing on me and missed. We
fought, and I beat him up; busted his nose. I was
known from then on as the one who had hands. I was
also known for braiding hair because I braided my
own hair every night until I was requested to braid
some of the other boy's hair. I eventually got moved
to a group home. While I was there, I was playing
basketball against one of the staff members and as I
was winning, I was talking crazy to him because that's
what I was accustomed to. When we later had our
daily meetings, the staff member said I needed anger
management, I was too aggressive, and I wasn't ready
to go home. She asked me how I felt about his

statement, and I responded that I needed to go home because I felt like my life was in danger. I brought up an issue that would counteract his statement.

There was a female staff member that would always play around with us like one of the guys.

One day she said, "Don't make me go to the trunk and get the pistol."

We egged her on telling her that she didn't really have one, but she went to her car and came back with the gun. We were all laughing as she waved the gun at us. I brought this incident up. They tried to get me to expound upon what I was referring to but I was only willing to talk to my case worker. The police came and I told them what happened, and my case worker came a few days later. In between time, one of the guys told the female staff member that I told on her and she began picking on me and mistreating me. She called me numerous bitches and hoes, and tried to get me to run. She told the guys if they wanted to jump me, they could jump me. She did everything she could to get to me before my caseworker showed up.

When my caseworker came to get me, I asked what was going to happen. He told me that he filed something with the judge, and if I could pass a lie detector test, I'd be going home, and if I failed the test, I was going to be sent back to the detention center until I was nineteen. They took me into the facility, the conductor explained how the test worked, and I passed the test. My caseworker took me straight home. I got to go home fifteen to twenty days earlier because of what happened in the group home.

Once I was out, I was seventeen and I got my first job at KFC. We moved to Rudolph. My sister started coming back around for the first time, and we started getting close and building a sibling bond and relationship. This is when I spun out of control having sex. When I went to go see my baby for the first time, Michelle and I started sleeping together. Aside from Michelle, I had sex with anyone I could lay on; older women, younger women, women in Clarksville, women in Nashville, anybody. Once, on my seventeenth birthday, I slept with my Michelle, went to Nashville to sleep with the girl I met in Nashville, then went to Clarksville to sleep with someone I was messing with there, and then headed back to Springfield and slept with Michelle again.

I started sleeping with older women too. I had a crush on this woman who had a big butt, and she'd always make comments like she'd rape me if I was old enough. I went to her house one night. She lived right across the street from my granny, so I parked my car at my granny's and walked over there. She took the time and taught me how to have sex. I was trying to thrust really fast, and she told me to slow down, and talked to me. I was seventeen and she was at least thirty-two. There was another older lady I had a crush on who did hair. I got her number from meddling in someone else's phone. I called her a few times and played on her phone, and then I finally told her who I was. She invited me over. When I walked in, she was naked underneath the robe she had on, and she untied it so I could see everything. I walked up to her and hugged her, and she grabbed my penis. I just knew I was going to sleep with her that night, but she said I couldn't stay because of her kids. One of her kids was in the grade behind me.

A couple days later we slept together, and I found myself at her house all the time sleeping with her. One day while we were sleeping together, I heard a knock on the window. I asked who it was, and she just brushed it off like it was nobody. I got up to put my pants on and her child's father kicked the door in and came around the corner as I was pulling my pants up. She told him to get out of her house, and he took the beer he was drinking and busted her in the head. She fell to the ground, so I hurried to finish putting my pants on, and put my shirt on. As I was leaving, he hit her in her head again. I just got in the car and drove off. She wouldn't stop calling me afterwards, but I kept trying to get rid of her. I lied and said my mom was going to press charges for statutory rape if she didn't stop harassing me.

I kept sleeping around. Every day was a different woman. It got to the point where I couldn't even sleep in the bed by myself. I feel like my molestation affected the way I viewed sex. Once I started having sex and lost Michelle, together those encounters triggered what was dormant in me for all that time. I didn't smoke, drink, or do drugs. Sex was my vice and that's all I wanted to do all day.

Around this time, my brother had the city sold out and was one of the biggest dope boys. Our dad put him on with somebody he used to be locked up with. He had money and cars and everything. I was only seventeen and still didn't really understand what was going on. I was living off the hype of my brother being the man. He never gave me anything or bought me anything since he went away the first time, so I decided to steal some dope from one the houses he stashed it. This was my first-time seeing dope and being able to identify what it was. I knew right then what I saw in the pantry as a child was the same thing. People always stopped me and told me to pass messages to my brother about what they needed. One day someone told me to tell my brother they needed a ball. I questioned what he meant and he told me three point five. I went and found his stash, put something on the scale that weighed what the person told me, and went to go sell it to him. Somebody stopped me to tell me to remind my brother that he still needed that ball. I told him I had it. I stole another one and sold it. He gave me a hundred dollars for it, so I made $200.

My brother caught wind that I was selling dope because the lady whose house he was stashing it, told him I was in and out. Plus, people told him they had already been served by me, so he called me over to the house. He weighed his dope, and saw that some was missing, so he went off because he wanted his money back. I gave him his two hundred dollars and left. DLo called me because he knew we could steal some dope from a guy named Brandon and he was away from his house at a dice game. We stopped at Peanut's house to plan it out, and he decided to come with us and be the look out. I called someone at the dice game to verify that he was there, and I told him to let me know if he left. We went to Brandon's house and kicked the door in. We ransacked his house, turning mattresses and dressers, and emptying shoe boxes. We finally found the dope in a shoe box under the bed. I put it in my pocket, and we left.

None of us knew anything about selling dope. My friend told me to take it to someone named Gee.

Gee told us he'd cook it for us and he told me how much he'd charge. When he weighed it all out, it was seven and a half ounces. He was the one who taught me the game. He told me how to weigh it, how much a gram cost, how much a ball, quarter, half, and whole cost. I had around $5000 worth of dope. I fronted him an ounce and he told me in two to three days, he'd have me a $1000. I had ample clientele because I was giving away extra when people bought something, and they all thought that I took it from my brother and just wanted to make some money. Then rumors started circulating that I robbed Brandon, so I took an AK47 that my brother kept under his truck and went back to Brandon's house. DLo, Peanut, and I all went together. I was driving, DLo was holding the AK47 in the passenger seat, and Peanut was in the back.

I asked Brandon if he was telling people I robbed him, even though I did.

He told me, "Lil Boo I didn't tell people that, people around me were telling me that because they know how you get down. I honestly don't know who it was."

I told him I didn't want to hear any more about me robbing him, and if I did, there was going to be some problems. He didn't want any trouble. I told him I had some work if he needed it, and he said he needed a zip which is two ounces, so I sold him two ounces of his own dope back to him right there. I had money but being young I blew through it quick.

One of the few times I actually went to school, I had in school suspension. I was sitting there and a white boy came up to me and told me he heard that we were hitting licks, which is robbing people, and if I could tell him whether or not he could pull off a heist he planned, he'd give me $5000, and the three other people he was doing the heist with would give me $5000 a piece too. He wouldn't give any information aside from the plan. I told him based off what he told me, it sounded like the plan would work. The woman was elderly and could hardly hear or see. The plan was for someone to watch the woman, two people go in and take a safe that held all the money, while another person stayed in the truck. It was a four-man job.

The day came when they decide to rob the woman, and he called me and told me he needed me to go because one of his people fell through. He needed me to be the fourth man because it would only work with four people. He gave me all the details, and told me it was $250,000 in a safe that they were stealing. I immediately agreed. They came to pick me up and I made up my own plan to have Peanut, Jeff and another friend, Terrell, steal the safe. When we went in, I acted like the safe was too heavy and we needed to leave to go get an extra person. We left and they dropped me off back at my house while they went to go find a fifth person. Terrell and Peanut came to pick me up and we went to steal the safe. We got in and out in thirty seconds. They dropped me back off at my mom's house, and went to go sit at the basketball court until I gave them the word. The white boys came to pick me back up. When we got back in the woman's house, they saw the safe was missing, and I turned it on them. I pulled the gun out and told them I wasn't leaving until I got my cut. I made it seem like they came to get the safe behind my back when they dropped me off. I kept the gun on them the whole ride back to my house and kept circling the same conversation about them setting me up.

When they left, we spent hours trying to get the safe open. I finally got a portion open and pulled out some of the money, about $5000 in all hundred-dollar bills. I reached back in and pulled out another $10,000. Michelle was living with me at the time because when I saw her walking down the street shortly before, I saw she was upset so I stopped and asked her what was going on. She told me she got into it with her mom and didn't want to live there anymore. I invited her and our daughter to come live with me. Michelle was in the kitchen with my daughter. I ran past them saying, "I got it!" I ran upstairs to my brother and told him, "I got it!" We both ran downstairs and he saw all the money.

He asked me, "What did you do?"

I told him, "I told you I got it."

We counted all the money, and it was $125,000 on the nose. My brother reached for the money, and Peanut pulled the gun on him because he wasn't with us when we went to go get the safe.

My brother picked up the money anyways and threw it in the air and said, "We're rich! We're back straight!"

My brother had just been robbed for the first time a month prior for $20,000. We decided to give him $60,000 so he could flip it and bring back more money, I took $40,000, and the rest of them split what was left. The next day the paper came out about this being the biggest robbery. The white boys got charged for it, but my name started coming up. The detective called me and told me he wanted to see me. I went down to the station and the detective believed that I couldn't have done it because I didn't know anything about it, the location, what time everyone went to work, etc. He believed they were just trying to put it on me because I had a bad reputation. After a fifteen-minute conversation, he let me go. The detective called me back and wanted to see me again.

He told me that he was informed that the white boys called me and told me everything that I needed to know to steal the safe, and that the phone records were going to be pulled. He asked me if he pulled the records, would he find that we'd been in contact with each other. I told him no because I was sticking with my story all the way through.

The detective called me a third time because he had the phone records. He asked me why they called me and informed me that they all had come clean about the entire thing. I threw them under the bus and told him they approached me in in school suspension and told me I'd get $5000 a piece from all of them if I could tell them if their plan would work or not. I told him I didn't see a dime of the money. He began asking me about my car and the nice coat I had on, but I stuck with my story, and he let me go. He called me a fourth time. I answered and told him that my mom said she was going to get him for harassment if he called me again because I went down there three times and got questioned as a juvenile with no adult supervision, and I hung up the phone. I never heard anything else about the case aside from rumors and accusations.

My brother never came through on his word about the $60,000 I gave him. We got into an argument one day because I had on his pants, and I reminded him that it was me who bought everything we had because of the lick *I* hit. He didn't care, he just wanted me to take his pants off. I went in my mom's room crying because I was hurt that my brother didn't come through on his end of the bargain, and I blew through my money on people, clothes, and cars, and studio equipment, because Michelle was a rapper and I thought that was something we could do together. I told her what happened. She asked me what I did with the money.

The first thing she said was, "You stupid! You should've gave the money to me!"

I talked to my dad and he told me I could take my last $1500 and he'd connect me with one of his dope connections, and I officially entered the dope game.

While my dad was setting up a plug connection, there was this girl named KeKe. Everyone around town said she was fine and good looking, but I never saw her before. Jeff had a crush on her, and one day we were riding around, we stopped on her street, and our friend we ran into was trying to convince Jeff to go talk to her because she already knew that he liked her. She was about twenty-six years old, and we were still seventeen. We pulled up to her house, and Jeff was inside talking to her. I was plotting on how to get inside so I could see what she looked like. I walked up to the door and knocked as I walked in.

She said, "who the hell are you walking up in my house like that?"

I responded, "Who are you?"

She replied, "I live here."

I told her my name and she hit me with the line most people use when they hear my name, "Oh you that crazy ass boy everybody be talking about... the one that shot at my cousin."

She was referring to a time I found out an older guy was trying to talk to my Michelle, and I found out, called my uncle, and did a drive by with an AK 47. I shot through his car six or seven times, and someone standing outside the car talking to him got hit in the ankle, which was her cousin. I denied it, and told her I didn't do it. We sat on the couch and started having a conversation. When we left, Jeff was saying how he was going to get her, but I was thinking to myself, "Nah, I'm going to get her." A few days later I was driving, and passed by her house as she was checking her mailbox. One of my friends that was riding with me bet me twenty dollars that I couldn't get her phone number. We pulled up to her house, and my friend that bet me did all the talking, telling her how I was interested in her.

She denied interest saying, "I don't wanna talk to that crazy ass nigga."

We all sat there talking and joking. Before we left, she put her number in my phone. My friend gave me my twenty dollars.

When I initially called her, we only talked briefly. After that, she stopped answering her phone, I assume because she recognized my number. I saw her niece walking down the street one day and told her, "Man tell your auntie to pick the phone up." She eventually answered the phone, and I went to her house one night to chill. It was getting late, and she kept mentioning that she had to go to work in the morning. That was her way of hinting that I needed to leave. I came back a couple of days after that and we ended up sleeping together. The next day she told me to lock the door and put the key under the rug when I left. When she left and went to work, I got up and went to my mom's house, grabbed everything I owned, clothes, shoes, studio equipment, *everything*, and took it to her house. When she came home from work, I had everything set up, my clothes hung up in the closet, put up in the drawers, studio equipment in the pantry, and shoes lined up at the bottom of the bed. She walked in her room, turned around, and walked right back out.

She said, "That's what I wanted you to do anyways."

I officially moved in with her. Then life *really* got crazy.

Chapter 5: The Storm

After I moved in with her, a week later, I sat on the couch and she warned me about her niece. She must've noticed something because she didn't want me around her. Her niece was fast and we were the same age, but she was coming to let her stay because she didn't want to stay in Nashville. Her niece was doing the dishes in some booty shorts. To me that was her signaling that she was ready. I went up behind her she jumped like she was rejecting me but, then she told me to let her get in the shower first. We slept together in KeKe's bed.

Back on the streets, my dad told me he connected me with Cike. Cike told me if I came up with $1400, he was going to get me straight, and take care of me. I sold my car for $1400 and I sold the sound system in my car for $700. I sold my keyboard from my studio equipment to the pawnshop for $1000. I took the $1400 to Cike and he gave me two ounces of dope. I came home and called Gee and he cooked up one ounce and left the other as cocaine. I was getting the dope off so fast that I went back with another $1400 every Friday. After a few times, one day Cike told me to meet him and not to bring any money. We were sitting in the car and he gave me the real OG dope man talk. He wanted to know how I handled and saved my money. He gave me his own saving method of how a $100 a day would lead to $3000 a month.

He lifted up the arm rest and asked, "Do you think you can handle that?"

"What is it?"

"It's four and a half, and I want $3000 for it."

I did the math and decided I could get it off quickly. So, I went from paying him $1400 to owing him $3000. After talking to Gee, I concluded that I could get this amount off for the amount Cike wanted me to, and still have an ounce left over for myself to do what I wanted with it. I went through the cycle of owing him $3000 about three times before he came to me and increased the amount from four and a half to a nine piece. He told me if I couldn't handle it, not to take it, because he wanted $6000 for it. I did the math in my head and decided it would be easy to sell, and at the rate I was selling it, I would have three ounces left over for myself to do what I wanted to do. So, I took the nine piece. I started getting back everything I lost. I went back and bought the same car I sold, I bought my sound system back, and my studio equipment. I bought a cutlass, and a dirt bike too, so I exceeded what I once had. I was in a good place.

I thought my brother was in a good place too, but he started falling off. He started whipping his own dope at that time so the quality wasn't as good which lead to his clientele falling off. He had a black Impala that he would never let me drive, but one day he came over and asked me to ride with him, and asked if I wanted to drive. This is the first time that I drove a car with a digital dashboard, I had a pocket full of money, I thought my brother had a pocket full of money, I felt good. My brother was just smoking and chilling as I drove without saying anything, so I told him I was just going to go back to the house. I pulled back up to the drive way and parked the car.

My brother leaned up, punched the dashboard, and started crying. I asked him what was going on.

He looked up and said, "I don't have anything left but $13,000."

I asked him why and he started explaining, but his story was all over the place, and I just thought it was impossible because I remember going under his bed and seeing $100,000 cash at one point and not only that I gave him $60,000. He then told me that his plug cut him off, and wasn't giving him any work. He asked me to talk to Cike, so I told him I would. I got out the car and went inside, and told KeKe what was going on. She advised me against it, but I told her he was my brother and I had to look out for him. I talked to Cike and he told me that he'd help my brother out, and just to have him call. My brother called, but I was unaware that he didn't even have the $13,000 that he claimed to have. I found out when I went to see Cike, he gave me half a bird which is two nine pieces, and told me to give my brother half; nine a piece, which meant we both owed him.

I was still hitting licks at the time because nothing ever seemed like enough. Greed was pumping in my veins. Flip came to my house one time and asked me to hit a lick with him because he had a lot going on and needed the money. I told him I'd find something, so I found a white boy who was selling weed. I went to Flip's house and he was in the back with his girlfriend. While I was watching a music video, I heard them in the back scuffling like they were fighting. They said some choice words, and he came to the front with his shirt hanging half off, and told me let's go. He didn't say anything when we got in the car, so I asked him when we got to the stop sign, "Man, I know you weren't in there fighting that girl."

"Man, she tripping. There was forty dollars on the dresser and I grabbed it and said I needed it, and she wasn't having it and jumped on me. That's what I'm saying man, I need this."

I called Peanut right then to set up the lick on the white boy. The plan was for Peanut to call for three pounds of weed, have him show up, and we rob them. Peanut told him he didn't have the money on him and he needed to go to his house to get it, so the white boys picked him up to take him to the house. We followed them and I text Peanut to get in on one side of the car, and get out on the other side to make sure both car doors were unlocked. He did that, and Flip and I got in the car with an AK 47 and 9mm in Peanut's driveway.

Peanut said, "Man you set me up!"

I reached over and smacked him in the mouth, "Man, shut up!" We were all in the back seat laughing because that wasn't a part of the plan. We took the book bag full of weed, we ran everyone's pockets, and then I got too excited and told them to take us to the house where all the weed was. Flip and Peanut gave me a look questioning what I was doing. I was determined to get all of it. They put the car in reverse and they started revealing who's weed it was, and how they were scared of the consequences they'd have to face for the weed coming up missing. I didn't care about any of that. We pulled up to the house, and I told the driver to go get the weed, and leave his friend in the passenger seat. I instructed him if he didn't comply or come back, we'd kill his friend and leave him in the car. The driver got out, but took a while to come back, so I was constantly checking to see when he'd come back around the corner. I saw a shadow and a gun coming around the corner so I jumped in the driver's seat, put it in reverse, backed up, and put the gun to the passenger's head.

He started crying, "Man, please don't kill me! Man, they're going to kill me!"

"Call in there and tell your friend to bring the weed and leave it at the mailbox or we're going to kill you and dump you in the river."

He called his friend crying, cussing him out, telling him he hated him and he was going to get him killed, and to bring the weed out. We turned the car around and saw the bookbag sitting at the mailbox, but we also saw the police. As soon as the police passed us, they cut their lights on. I smashed the gas, Flip and I jumped out the car, but Peanut had to stay. Jeff lived in the area, so we ran to his house. I had on basketball shorts under my jeans, and a white shirt under my black shirt. I stripped my outer outfit and threw it in the trash, and hid everything I just stole from them under Jeff's storage bin in his back yard. I don't know where Flip ran to, but I walked to the end of the street dribbling Jeff's basketball. The police rolled past and asked me if I saw anything suspicious going on in the neighborhood. I said that I didn't, and they left. I sat on the porch and waited for KeKe to come get me. When she pulled up, Flip jumped out the car. I don't know how he ran across town that fast, but she already picked him up. We got in the car and he showed me three pounds of weed. I went and got the rest from under the storage bin in the back yard. We went to my house and discussed how we were going to sell it and what we were going to do.

I quit going to school completely, so I was on the run for truancy. I was riding with DLo and another guy. We pull over one day and a woman walked up and asked for a forty; she wanted some dope. My friend and I look at each other and are in agreement that this lady is the police. DLo didn't care and wanted to make the sale. He got out, walked to her car, reached in his pocket like he was going to serve her, and when she pulled out the forty dollars, he snatched her money and told her to pull off. She pulled off, and he got back in the car with us and we pulled off. We rode up the street and saw the police on the far end of the street. DLo pulled in the driveway like he was going to knock on someone's door, and as soon as we parked, the police flew down the street and pulled in right behind us. I jumped out the car, and got away. I ran to my cousin's house to use her phone to call KeKe to come get me. I didn't know that an undercover agent saw me standing next to the house, so he approached me with a gun on me and told me to put my hands up.

The officer said, "You've been on the run for a while haven't you Baker?"

He cuffed me and called for a police car to come and get me. The police car came, took me down to the police department, and my case worker came and got me. He transported me to DCS custody and he told me I was going to a hick town detention center for temporary placement. He advised me not to playing with the people up there because there were rumors of them being racist. I asked him why was he taking me if they were racist, but he said it was the only temporary placement they had for me at the moment. It was a four-hour drive to a really small building with two cells that could only hold four men and two women. There was a small old man working there, and I was going to be staying for two days. During those two days, I heard the cell door open, but I initially didn't turn over because I was mad about being caught. When I did turn around, I saw it was Flip who was also on the run.

He said, "What's up Joe?"

"Man, what are you doing here?"

"Man, they caught me at the gas station."

I could smell him from where I was, and told him, "Man, you need to shower."

"For real bruh?" he walked over to the corner of the cell, pulled down his pants, looked at his underwear, looked up at me and said, "Man I got shit stains from here to Mississippi!"

He had my dying laughing. As we were sitting there, he was telling me the details of how he got caught, and how he was going to do the time. After a few days in the cell, I told him I was going to escape. He asked me how I planned to do that, so I told him I'd have someone drive up, knock on the door, and when they opened the door, beat up the guard, take his keys, and get me out. I used the phone to call the people I wanted to get me out, and told them what to do and how to do it, assuming no one was listening. As we were watching TV one night, they unplugged the TV. The guard unlocked the cell and asked me to step out. Four of the officers took me to the kitchen, a woman, an older man, and two very large officers that looked like they worked out daily. I sat at the table, and one of the officers approached me to ask me if I knew the names of the people I mentioned on the phone. I denied knowledge of them. He told me that they caught the names he mentioned. I asked him what that had to do with me.

"So, they weren't on their way here to break you out, and jump on my officer, and let you out of your cell?"

"Man, I don't have a clue what you're talking about."

"Your phone calls are recorded. We know you called and said those things."

I still denied knowledge of what they were talking about. So, he grabbed my arm.

"You calling me a liar boy?"

His voice changed and everything. He got real country and real racist. I got scared and told him to get off me.

"You calling me a liar nigger?"

He grabbed me with his other hand and choked me and picked me up out of the chair as the other officer grabbed my other hand. I struggled to break free to defend myself and he punched me in my face twice. I start calling for Flip to come help me.

The lady yelled out, "That's enough!"

She stopped it and they put me back in the cell. I had bruises on my neck and my face. I told them I wanted to call my caseworker the next morning and they allowed me to call.

I told him what happened and the first thing he said was, "I told you not to go up there messing with those folks."

"No, you should've never brought me up here! I want to call my momma!" He told me he would send transportation to come pick me up, and in between time they took me to the doctor and took pictures to document what happened. Transportation came and took me to Lebanon where we would meet my case worker. We pulled up at DCS and they asked me if I wanted to go to the bathroom. On the way there I saw these projects I intended on running to, so I said yes. We got out the car and while we were all walking to the bathroom, I stopped and let them keep walking. When they turned around to tell me to come on, I took off running down the street to the projects. A group of guys were standing outside, and when I approached them, I told them that I just ran from DCS custody and just needed to use the phone to call someone to come get me. They told me they just had

94

someone run from there, so I was in good hands. I called KeKe and she called someone to come and get me. I wasn't even locked up four days before I got back home, so Cike never even knew what was going on. When I came home, I got back in the normal routine of things.

As things were back to normal, I was living with KeKe, but sometimes I'd switch it up and stay with my cousin Sherry, who would let me drive her car. I was driving her car one day on the way to go check on one of my cars in the shop, and I got a private phone call.

When I answered a woman said, "I can have you if I want you."

I found out it was Flip's girlfriend, Kay. He was still locked up and she was sitting on her grandmother's porch and saw me drive by. I told her to call me back with the number showing so I could call her back later because I was busy. I told DLo about it, and he told me that was another place that I could stay since I was on the run, so I started hanging with her. I went over her house the first few times and we didn't sleep together. One night I was staying all night and Flip called from prison while I was in the bed with her. I told her I was just going to leave and come back. While I was gone, she texted me and told me he wanted her to call me on three way. We all got on the phone, and all he wanted to know was what I was doing since I was out because he heard I was financially comfortable. I showed off by telling him all the moves I was making, the stuff I was buying, how successful I was being, and I sent him some money. I'm sure that only intrigued Kay even more.

My brother was still having problems getting money. I was at KeKe's house and he came over and told me how he got into with this guy. He was explaining what happened without being specific so I just told him we could handle it in the morning.

He said, "Man you acting like a little bitch."

"Who?"

"You got you some little money, and your own plug, and I tell you somebody shot Momma's car, and you acting like you don't wanna ride. You acting like a little bitch."

"Who shot Momma's car?" He told me his name and it was his friend that he hung with. I told him let's go so he could show me my mom's car. When we got there, my brother's car was parked across the street. I wondered why the guy would shoot my mom's car if my brother's car was right across the street. He showed me the hole in my mom's car, and I assumed it was a bullet hole because of what my brother told me. I immediately thought that guy had to die. My brother, Terrell, and I start riding around looking for him. I had a 9mm and pocket full of bullets. We come to a four way with the guy who shot the car. Terrell was driving, my brother was in the passenger seat, and I was in the back. My brother got down like he was scared and told us those were the guys. I got out the car with my hand behind my back, and the car door blocking the gun so they couldn't see it. I throw my other hand in the air to signal, "What's up?" They turned their lights on bright. I didn't know what that meant so I started shooting in the car. When I ran out of bullets I got back in the car.

My brother said, "Nigga you gangsta for real."

"Nigga shutup, they done shot Momma car up, what you mean?" I started loading the clip back up and Terrell started riding in reverse. He said we had to go park the car because I just got done shooting, but I told him no, and to follow their car. We chased them down, but we could never get close enough for me to let off any more shots. They turned the corner and I told my Terrell to go park because they could've been standing around the corner waiting. I later found out that whole situation was about my brother messing with that guy's girlfriend. So, I never really knew if the hole in my mom's car was a bullet hole or not.

There were situations where people owed my brother money, and he'd send me to get it. He called me one day and told me a guy owed him $5000. I pulled up on the guy, and said, "Aye, my brother sent me to get that money."

"I'm going to pay him today."

"My brother sent me over here to get it."

"It's cool, me and him already talked about it."

I got out the car and walked over to his car. "We can go get the money right now, or I'll take it out your pockets."

"Man don't come over here with all that tripping."

"I'm not tripping, I'm just doing what my brother asked me to do." We rode to his house and got the money. Now that guy had a problem with me. It seemed like there were multiple situations like that. In another instance, my brother had a guy cooking his dope for him. He thought he was trying to play him by pouring the dope down the drain because the dope came up short, so when he told me what was going on, I told him let's go get it. We went to the spot, and there were about six guys standing outside. I cocked and pointed my gun at the guy my brother was referring to, and my brother patted him down. He asked him where his dope and his money were. He told him he was tripping, and the dope wasn't any good, so he lost out. I looked in the house and it was a house full of dope boys. The woman who lived in the house pleaded with me not to come in there with "that gun stuff" because her kids were in the bed sleep, and they had to get up and go to school the next day. I told her to shut up and proceeded to tell them my brother came up short and somebody needed to come up with his dope. They all said they didn't have anything to do with it, but I told them if somebody didn't come up with his dope that I was going to rob everybody. They all pitched in and came up with the dope, so we took it and left. Now I had a problem with all of them. Most of my problems were coming from people owing my brother money, and he not having the heart to go get what they owed him.

It seemed like everything was crazy. I was on the run, stuff with my brother, stuff with money, stuff in the streets, sleeping with multiple women. It got to the point where I started sleeping with my cousins. Kresha lived walking distance from KeKe, the same cousin I grew up with that I used to have a crush on.

I'd go to her house to stay sometimes when I wanted
to switch it up since I was on the run. I'd sleep on her
couch, but I still didn't like sleeping alone, so I'd wake
up in the middle of the night and go get in the bed
with her. One night I was in the bed with her and I
rolled over to hold her, but I went inside her as I did
it. We slept together, and when she got up for work
the next morning, she warned me not to tell anyone
about what we did. She was best friends with my
child's mother, Michelle, too, so not only would it be
frowned upon because we were family, but because I
was the father of her best friend's baby. After that we
started sleeping together here and there.

DLo was dating my cousin Tracy at the time
and she would let me stay at her apartment. She
would always say things like if you weren't my cousin,
I'd do this and that to you. Sherry's sister had an
apartment she didn't want anymore, so she let me
have the apartment. One night around midnight I
called her and told her lets go chill at the apartment. I
went and picked her up and we went to the apartment
and just hung out. I started feeling on her and took
her by the hand and led her in the back room. We

started sleeping together using protection, but one time the condom broke, and I just kept going.

Another cousin would say she wanted to do things to me. I was over her house watching TV and she asked me for the remote so she could watch what she wanted to watch. I wouldn't give her the remote, so she told me she knew how to get it from me. I thought she was going to play wrestle and try to get the remote from me, but she started unbuttoning my pants and performed oral sex on me. That led to us having sex on the couch. Things like this just made me feel like my life was spiraling out of control and I didn't know how to get a hold on it.

When Kay and I started sleeping together, she wanted me to leave KeKe and move in with her. KeKe and I were on rocky ground because she was upset about me constantly going to stay with Sherry. She wanted me at home with her. Rumors started circulating that KeKe was entertaining DLo. When I heard that, I cut KeKe off. One day DLo and I were riding around, and we saw KeKe with Peanut, who was one of my closest cousins, parked on the corner where everybody usually sold their drugs. The corner had a small crowd with everyone just hanging out. As soon as I got out the car, Peanut and KeKe got out the car, and KeKe immediately started explaining that she was just trying to get my new phone number and find out where I was staying because I hadn't been in contact. I ignored her and addressed Peanut.

Peanut and I never had any problems, I let him hold my money, I fronted him dope, we hit licks together, and did mostly everything together. I asked him what was up and asked if he was trying to get with KeKe and he didn't respond. I told him to just give me my money and my dope. He still didn't respond, he just stood there mugging me. I asked him again, and he didn't respond, he just stood staring, still mugging me. I walked up to him and asked him if he wanted to fight me based off the way he was looking at me, and he *still* didn't respond. I reached over and smacked him, he still stood without a response. I smacked him again and said, "If you want to fight me, go ahead and try to fight me." Still no response. I reached over a third time and smacked him, he took his shirt off and rushed towards me. I moved, hit him two or three times, and he was in a daze. While he was in a daze looking around, I cocked my fist all the way back and hit him in his temple and split his eye open. He fell to the ground, and when he got up, he asked one of the guys standing there if he could use his phone. He grabbed the phone, and without dialing out, he put the phone to his ear and started talking. It worried me so I went over to him and grabbed him and shook him. He looked at me, took a step back, reached in his pocket for my money, and my dope, and he threw it on the ground. I reached down and grabbed it and told him to get in the car.

He said, "I'm not going anywhere with you, you ain't straight."

"What you mean I ain't straight? You were the one in the car with *my* girlfriend." He then tried to explain, but I told him he should've said that first. I turned around and looked at her and she took off running. I chased her down, grabbed her by her hair and dragged her back to the car. I told her to get in the car and leave, so she left. I got back in the car

104

with DLo and told Peanut to get in the car with me. We went out to the apartment and talked. I apologized and told him he wasn't right for that. After everything was resolved, DLo and I left to go drop off Peanut. I got a phone call afterwards from someone telling me that DLo was the one messing with KeKe. I still didn't pay it any attention.

After that incident, KeKe and I started sleeping together again, but we still weren't on the best of terms. One day, I went to KeKe's house to get some money I left in a shoebox. DLo and I pulled up and I told her to bring it out. She brought it out with an attitude and threw it in the car. It fell down to the side with my gun, so I leaned down to get it, and when I got back up, she winked. I didn't think anything of the wink, I just thought she was being her silly self. I looked at him and he was laughing, and I assumed he was laughing because she was being silly. I kept getting a lot of different people telling me they were messing around, but I refused to believe it because he was my ace and we grew up together. Even after seeing that, my mind wouldn't accept that he would do that.

I went to go see my plug, Cike, and on my way back KeKe called me and told me to come behind the projects because she had something to show me. I told her we both knew I didn't ever go back there for any reason, but she told me DLo was back there and he was going to tell me they were in love. They didn't know I was in Kay's car, and the car had tinted windows, so I went behind the projects and parked. There were about thirty guys outside standing around. She kept calling and texting my phone, so I finally answered.

She said, "Come back here behind the projects."

"I'm already here, I've been here." I flashed my lights so she could see me.

"Oh, that's that bitch car, so you are fucking with that bitch! Does your homeboy know? I'm going to tell him!" She rolled her window down to tell DLo to come to the car.

I pulled up closer, and she told him to tell me how they were in love. I said, "What's up cuz, you messing with her?"

"Man, I don't know what that bitch talking about, I don't even mess with her like that."

"Man, if you want her you can have her." I lifted up the dope I just bought. "I'm getting money. What ya'll got going on don't got nothing to do with me, but you ain't getting shit from me." I pulled off. She called me trying to argue, but I didn't care. She tried to embarrass me in front of a bunch of people. I went back to Kay's house because she had to go to work that night. KeKe was still blowing my phone up, but I stopped answering. She texted me that she was going to send the police over to Kay's because she knew I was on the run. I knew she was bluffing.

Kay's brother was there with me and we heard someone bang on the door. I looked out the window and it was the police. Her brother was a junky and he was high. He was panicking saying he had to open the door, but I kept telling him, we were just going to act like nobody was home. He headed

107

towards the door and said he was still going to open the door. I crawled to the hallway to stop him before he made it to the door and told him to come here. He came in the room, and I showed him the dope I just got. I said, "You either don't answer the door or you answer the door and say you're on your way to work and you're running late, but nobody else is in the house. If you do that, I'll give you some of this."

"How much are you going to give me?

"I'll give you three grams."

He got up and went to the door and did exactly what I said and told them nobody was in the house. The police left, and he flew back to where I was and asked for his three grams. I called Kay to tell her what was going on and she left work early that night just to come back and chill with me. KeKe was still blowing my phone up with details about me messing with Kay, times I got dropped off, and what we were doing. She even knew about me messing with a girl named Johnny. DLo dropped me off at Johnny's house, and DLo was the only one who knew she was there. I found out it was DLo who was telling

KeKe everything, both trying to use it as leverage, and to let KeKe know it was safe for them to sleep around. One day he dropped me off at Kay's house and KeKe showed up asking where I was because she knew I was there. I laid back really low in the seat so she couldn't see me. She started going off, cussing Kay out.

"He was with me last night eating my pussy and eating my ass! So, when you kiss him, you eating my pussy and eating my ass too!"

I leaned up in the chair and said, "When?"

When she saw me, she said, "I knew you was out here! I knew you were fucking with that bitch!"

I decided I didn't need neither one of them. I got out the car and started walking up the street. I turned to see KeKe's Mustang flying up the street trying to run me over. I jumped in the grass and called Sherry to come and get me. I didn't mess with Kay too much after that because I didn't want to risk anything with the police. I wanted to stay free, stay low, and get money. It kind of cut me deep that DLo would do that because this was the first person I ran a train on a girl with. I used to spend the night over his house and everything. We had history. This is who I was fronting most of my work to. He had a gambling problem, so if he wanted me to hold his money I would. If anybody knew all my secrets, it was him.

Regardless, money didn't stop for feelings so I never stopped trying to get money. I was putting together a lick to hit where I was hoping to hit at least a quarter million. A lot of people talked about it, but I was determined to actually do it. This guy named Don had a routine every morning; he'd drive to three gas stations and then go to work. The plan was when he parked his car to go to work, we'd kidnap him, take him to a hotel that we'd put in someone else's name, have him call his girlfriend and have her bring the money to the park. He was one of the biggest dope boys in Springfield. Nobody knew about this plan except Peanut who I was plotting with. I rode down the street where Don lived, and I passed one of my cousins who flagged me down. He told me I needed to go talk to Don. I got in the car with my cousin because he was friends with the Don, and he took me down there. I'm stood in the driveway and Don came down with a pistol in his basketball shorts.

He said, "If you say it ain't nothing, we'll squash it right now in this yard."

"What are you talking about?"

"I know somebody has been following me to work. I have a certain routine that I do, and the person who told me about this knew my routine. The only way anybody would know my routine is if somebody was following me to work."

He ended up telling me my entire plan about kidnapping him for a ransom. I was racing in my mind because I knew Peanut would not have done that. I thought back to a big guy named Cody that approached me, asking to get in on my licks because his friends weren't dealing with him. I called Cody later to tell him the plan because I knew with him being bigger, he could grab Don in the kidnapping. I knew right then that Cody was the one that told Don.

Don said, "I respect what you do, I respect your hustle, I respect you hittin' licks, but I ain't the one. So, if you tell me right now that it's a dead issue, we'll leave it at that."

I looked at my cousin who gave me a look like, "Take him at his word." The only thing I was thinking was let me make it out this yard so I can go deal with the snitch. I told him it was a dead issue, and that there was nothing more to it.

He said, "Now, like I told you, I respect you. If you're hungry or you need something you can come holla at me, but I ain't the one. I gotta couple sandwiches in the fridge, you just can't have my steak."

I agreed and left. I immediately call Peanut and told him we had to go see about the snitch. I called the snitch and he didn't answer. I blew his phone up, but I kept getting his voicemail.

It said, "You have reached Cody. If you ain't no real nigga don't expect no call back from me, and don't leave me a message. If you is a real nigga, gon and leave me a message."

I left a voicemail that said, "No, you ain't no real nigga, and when I see you, I don't give a fuck where it's at, if it's in McDonald's drive thru, if it's the convenience store, the grocery store, I don't care if it's a church nigga, you tried to get me killed, and when I see you I'm going to deal with you on sight."

Not even five minutes later he called me boo ho crying.

He said, "Man I wasn't trying to do that man. I was messing with this girl and we were rolling off some X pills. There was a girl Don was messing with, but I didn't know he was messing with her like that. I was just telling her how you were going to help me out, and how I was going to hit a lick with you, and you were going to get me straight—"

I cut him off, "What the hell you mean? Why are you telling people my name or telling people who we're robbing? Just for you saying that, when I see you, I'm coming to get you." I hung up the phone. I didn't see him for a while after that, but he eventually came and brought me a pair of green and black see through Nikes to my mom's house, so we left it at that. I had all kinds of problems with everybody. I didn't hesitate to open fire and start shooting at people, whether they had beef with my brother or whether they owed me money.

It got so bad that I was at Sherry's house one day with Terrell and another friend. We were all laughing and kicking it. We got to the house, and Sherry asked me if I was okay, and I told her I was, but I really wasn't. I walked in the bathroom and backed up to the wall, and slid down the wall, crying. I just broke down. I was tired. I was on the run, I couldn't do anything, everywhere I went I had to have a gun. I had beef with what seemed like everybody. My life was completely out of control. At any given time, I had to run from the police or go to war with somebody. It was always something going on and I was tired. It was so bad that when I went to my momma's house at night, I had to circle through the entire back yard with my lights on bright just to make sure no one was there waiting on me. I would walk backwards with my back towards the door and my gun pointed out until I got in the door and locked it.

Whenever someone got robbed, everyone automatically assumed it was me, even if it wasn't.

When I came out the bathroom, Sherry looked at me and asked me if I had been crying. I told her the truth, that I didn't know what to do and I was tired. She told me to go turn myself in, but I couldn't do that. I had $10,000-15,000, I had guns, I had a secure plan of places I could go, things I could do, everything. I was just tired. She told me I had two options: keep doing what I'm doing, or turn myself in. I decided to keep doing what I was doing. I walked outside and got in the car with Terrell and my other friend like nothing happened and went to go drop them off.

Chapter 6: The Aftermath

I began thinking to myself that I was ready to turn myself in. I didn't drink but I thought to myself I was going to take a drink. Sherry and I went to the liquor store and I told her to grab me something because Gee wanted some. She came back with a fifth of Hennessey, and I went to go get in my car. While I was on the run, I always had Michelle's sister pump my gas. I would go get her, flirt with her, and she'd get out and pump my gas. Every time she got out the car, I'd smack her on her butt. While I was sitting at the gas station, KeKe text me asking to do something for her. I just saw my plug and got a new batch of dope that day. When I told KeKe that I couldn't do it, she got mad and told me she was going to flush my dope down the toilet. I blacked out.

I went to the house and walked in with my gun in my hand. Her son was in the front yard playing and her mom was sitting on the living room couch. I went straight to the room where I kept my dope and saw it was gone. I walked back out and went to the kitchen where she was washing dishes. I pointed the gun at her and told her if she didn't tell me where my dope was, I was going to kill her right there.

Her mom came in pleading, "Boo, please don't shoot my child, please don't shoot my child."

Her mom kept trying to convince her to tell me where she put it. KeKe walked up to me, told me to pull the trigger and tried to spit on me. I turned around to look at her mom and I saw her son getting ready to open the door. I put the gun up. I told them not to worry about it, and they'd read about me. I reached in the pantry and grabbed my AK47 and got back in Sherry's car. I pulled off and while I was riding, I saw a guy I was beefing with from a distance. There were a lot of people outside, kids included. I told myself when I circle back around to the stop sign, I was going to spray anything I saw moving. When I turned the corner, DLo was running a stop sign and pulled up right in front of me. I thought to myself, "He's trying to play me too." I set the AK47 out on the window and just started shooting. I probably let off about fifteen shots. I shot through both his windows. His brother was in the passenger seat and tried to jump out the passenger window. DLo pulled off swerving, I thought I hit him because I saw his hood fly up. I pulled back on KeKe's street and flew up the street. I just remember thinking to myself how I didn't care, and I was going to kill anyone who was in my way. I came back around to the stop sign that mentioned. I had two magazine clips, sixty shots in each clip. I shot the AK47 for two minutes, just letting it fire off. I shot somebody three times.

My phone rang and my friend was telling me his granny heard my name come across the scanner so I might want to get low. I didn't want to, I wanted to get the guy I was beefing with and wanted to kill, not knowing that I already shot him three times. I came back around the corner and there was an undercover police officer. I noticed because when he saw me come around the corner, I saw him get really low in his seat. I smashed the gas. Police were coming from every direction as I led them on high speed chase. I had two guns, an ounce of dope, a scale, and a Pyrex jar, plus the fifth of Hennessey under my seat I never opened. The car started slowing down because I was running out of gas. After deciding against shooting at the police to slow them down, I found a place where I could jump out the car. I jumped out and took off running. I could see the police from a far distance. I jumped one fence, came to another, jumped that fence, and then my body completely shut down. I laid on the ground seeing the police officers run towards me wondering to myself why I couldn't move my body. The police came to me and asked what was wrong. I told them I couldn't move anything on my body. They didn't touch me; they just called an ambulance. I thought my body was paralyzed.

The ambulance came but because I was under arrest, they couldn't put me in the ambulance. They picked me up and placed me in the police car. They drove me to the hospital, and while we were on the way, I regained some activity of my limbs, enough to get the cocaine out of pocket and push it as deep down into the seat as possible. We got to the hospital and they walked me in. The doctor ran blood test on me and concluded that I was just low on potassium. They gave me some bananas and some water and told me I'd be fine. While I was sitting there, they rolled in the guy that I shot. He was shot twice in his arm and once in his upper thigh and buttocks area. They asked me was he the guy I shot, but I told them I didn't shoot anybody. They asked the guy if I was the one who shot him, and he said he didn't know who shot him. I said, "Well I guess I'll be leaving." I tried to get up and walk out. They told me I wasn't going anywhere because they found the gun that he was shot with in the car that I was driving. I told them I wasn't driving a car. They told me they didn't see anyone else jump out the car but me while they were chasing me. I said, "Well, I guess I'll be going to juvenile detention." They called my caseworker and transported me to a detention center.

I got there and they put me in a room, and asked me to take down my hair. At this time, I had braids in the front, and plats in the back. I started taking my hair down, but I stopped and decided I wasn't going to do it. The woman came back and asked me why I wasn't taking my hair down. I said, "I'm not taking down my mutha fuckin hair."

"Excuse me? What did you say? Are you being disrespectful?"

"I said I'm not taking down my mutha fuckin hair." At this point, I've already been through this and I already knew there wasn't much they could do to me. She left the room and came back with three men. "I don't know why the fuck you brought them in here, I'm still not taking my hair down, they don't scare me. You can call my caseworker in the morning." They picked me up and took me to the really small room where I could barely take three steps forward before I had to turn around. I sat in this room, and I thought about this charge, my money, the dope KeKe claimed she flushed down the toilet, the rumor going around that she was sleeping with my best friend, DLo, everything. My mind was all over the place. I had to get out of there and get back in the streets and finish my business. I told myself I was going to play crazy. When the woman came back around and looked in the room, she asked me what was wrong because I made it look like I was crying. I told her I was hearing voices.

She said, "What?"

"I'm hearing voices."

"What are they telling you?"

They're telling me to kill everybody around me or hurt myself."

She ran off and called this place called Mobile Crisis. They took me out of the small room and sat me down and asked me what was going on. They asked what voices I was hearing. I told them that the voices reminded me of my granddad's death. They asked me what happened. I told them that he was sick with cancer, and the last time I saw him, I beat him in a card game. A few days later my mom woke me up and told me I didn't have to go to school because my granddad died. He was one of the closest men in my life. I told them I felt like the devil was telling me that he was in hell, and my mother was a whore. I was making up all kinds of things that the voices were saying; telling me to kill people, and to kill myself. The woman made a report and told me she wasn't going to send me to the mental hospital that night, and that she thought I'd be okay. She told me she would have someone come out to check on me in the morning. They put me in a cell, and I'm thought about making that I pulled it off the next day because I had to get to the mental hospital.

When the morning came and they brought me my food, I was back in full character. I just stood staring at the ground with tears rolling down my face. The woman asked me if I was okay, and I didn't respond. Another officer came and yelled my name and kept repeating that nobody was in the cell but me. I looked at him and put my fingers up to my lips, and said, "Shhh." I looked back down at the ground. I had to stay in character while all the other kids were laughing. They took me out of the cell and placed me in a solitary room until Mobile Crisis came back. A different woman from the night before came and interrogated me about the voices I was hearing. She came in with a cup of water because I told them I got really thirsty when I heard the voices. As she questioned me, I didn't respond to anything she asked me. I finally looked up and told her, "Shhh." She asked me why and I reached for her paper and pen and wrote, "He's in here." Once she read it, she asked me who, but I told her "Shhh" again. I grabbed her paper again and wrote: "He's telling me to hurt myself or hurt other people." Instead of speaking, she wrote on the paper, "What's his name?" I wrote back "First Choice Johnny." She asked me why it was First Choice and I told her because whatever he tells me to do will be my first choice. She asked me was I going to hurt myself and other people. I told her I didn't want to, but he was telling me to. I finished my fourth cup of water and she asked me if I wanted another cup out loud instead of writing. I looked up with tears streaming down my face and told her, "He's in here." The woman grabbed everything she could as fast as she could and told the guards to let her out. When she went out, she told them to get me to the mental facility as fast as possible. I was transported that night.

I got to the facility and I was interrogated again and evaluated. When they finally took me to the room I was going to be sleeping in, I saw my roommate was a small white boy who had cuts all over his entire body. Anywhere he could cut had cuts;

his arms, legs, stomach everywhere was covered. I told them I was not going to stay in that room, and they told me it was the only bed they had available. I just went in the room and laid down because I was more concerned about escaping. When they shut the door, my roommate sat up and asked me my name. Without rolling over I told him my name. I was thinking about all the problems I had to solve once I got back home. He asked me why I was there, and I told him I was hearing voices. He got up out the bed intrigued.

He started walking towards me saying, "I'm going to kill you tonight Joe."

Every time he said it, he took a step closer to me. I wasn't scared, but I just thought to myself, "I'm going to have to hurt this boy." He was finally standing over my bed.

"I'm going to kill you tonight Joe."

I took the pillow, grabbed him and choked him out while I smothered him with the pillow. He was screaming and hollering into the pillow, and when I removed it, I asked, "You said you were going to do what?"

"I'm sorry! I'm sorry! I was just playing! I wanted to see if you were serious!"

I put the pillow back over his face and said, "Listen mutha fucka, you gon quit playing with me, I ain't the one to be playing with." I took the pillow off his face and pushed him. When I pushed him, he gasped for air and started apologizing.

Panting for air he said, "Man, I swear I'm sorry, I apologize. We have to get up in the morning for class, but we have to go get breakfast first. I'll get you up on time cause you don't want to be late cause you'll miss your breakfast, and we'll go to class. Do you need any toothpaste? Do you have a washcloth? Whatever you need I'm going to have it already out for you. I'm going to bed now."

He got in his bed and went to sleep. We got up the next morning and he did exactly what he said he was going to do. He had a washcloth out, let me use his toothpaste so I didn't have to use the state toothpaste, and gave me a brand-new toothbrush. I got myself together and he showed me where breakfast was. He introduced me to everybody else that was there who were literally out of their mind. I thought I was going to play crazy, but people really had issues. While we were at breakfast, I noticed this big guy had two staff members with him at all times. I asked my roommate what his deal was, and he told me he liked to hit people. I told him, "Well if he hits me, he's going to have a world of problems." As I'm saying that he reached over and smacked someone in the head. When he hit him, the guy who he hit tried to raise up to defend himself and the staff member stopped him. He could hit people and get away with it.

We finished breakfast and went to class. While we were in class, one of the students didn't want to participate. The staff member came in and tried to talk to him, but he got upset and lost it. They came in and tackled him, gave him a shot in his butt, put him in a vest and placed him in a padded room. We finished class and went to the day area where we could watch TV. We were all in agreement about what we wanted to watch. The two staff members bring in the big guy back in, and he said what he wanted to watch, and they changed the channel to what he wanted. He hit somebody again, and they restrained the person who he hit, and he got away with hitting someone again.

I'm scoped the place trying to figure out how to get out, and I didn't see a way. There were fences all over, and every door had a button. The entire place was secure. I found out that someone from Springfield was there and I found out it was my cousin. He told me to make sure I took my medicine and to be on good behavior to help with my case since I was being charged with attempted murder. A few days later my caseworker walked in. I asked him, "What are you doing here?"

He said, "Joe you don't need to be here, I've known you all your life and you don't need to be here. Pack your shit up, we're going back to the detention center, you're being discharged."

"I'm not going back there."

"You are tonight."

They packed my stuff up and took me back to the detention center. I argued with my caseworker the whole way there. When we got there, I didn't waste any time. I put on the same performance and told them the same thing about hearing voices. They sent the same woman back from Mobile Crisis, and I told her the same thing I told her the first time. She told me she didn't know how I ended up back in the detention center. She told me she was putting an emergency transfer on me and that would at least me keep me at the mental facility for thirty days. They packed my stuff up and I was on my way back to the mental facility the next day. I got back and all my little family was happy to see me. All the crazy folks were cool. There was a worker that I got cool with and he knew I wasn't crazy like the rest. I saw him texting one time and asked him to let me use his phone because I was tired of using the payphone. At night he'd come let me use his phone, and I'd be up all night texting.

One day they let us play basketball outside. There was a guy rapping, so I went over and listened to him rap, and he mentioned something about a key to the handcuffs while pulling a key out his pocket. When he finished rapping, I got cool with him and asked him where he got the key from. He wouldn't tell me, he just said that he was going to try to escape. He was supposed to be at the facility for a long time. I kept trying to convince him to give me the key because I was able to leave earlier, but he never gave me the key.

I was there for about eleven days before I saw my caseworker walking down the hall again. I threw my hands in the air as he smiled at me from a distance. He told me he was taking me back to the detention center because I wasn't crazy. I told him I had emergency transfer which meant I had to be there for at least thirty days under court order. He told me he already worked it all out and told them I wasn't crazy. They discharged me so I went to my room. Everyone came to my room asking me what was going on I told them I didn't know but my case worker had come to get me. I looked at the guy with the key and told him that was my only way out. I told him I'd come back and get him.

He said, "You'd come back and get me for real?"

I said, "If I have to steal a car and run through the room where you sleep at so you can run out of here, I'll do it. Just give me the key."

"I believe you."

He went to his room, got the key and came back and handed it to me. I put the key under my tongue. I followed my caseworker out with my stuff, and we got in the van. He put me in the back row. As we rode, he asked me if I was hungry, I told him I was, so we stopped at Wendy's. He asked me what I wanted. I spit the key in my hand and told him a number six, spicy chicken, add cheese and bacon, and a lemonade to drink. As we left, I bent down to take one of the shackles off my ankle. It unlocked so I knew the key worked and I got excited. I took that shackle and put it on my other ankle, but they didn't hear anything because the music was turned up and I would cough when I clicked it so they couldn't hear the lock. We got to the detention center, my caseworker was writing the mileage down, and the other guy in the passenger seat told me to get out the van while he held my stuff. I acted like I still had the shackles on both ankles, but it was only on one. By the time my feet hit the ground, I took off running with my hands cuffed, the shackles on one ankle, and the key under my tongue. I suppose the guy didn't pay much attention assuming I still had the shackles on, and I wouldn't get far. When he finally looked up, I was down the street. He yelled for me not to run. I took off across the highway in front of all the cars. I went to this car shop where they were hooking up speakers and asked to use the phone. I called KeKe and told her to come and get me. I told her I was in Murfreesboro, so she said they were on the way. I walked to a center that was similar to the YMCA and they were still inside playing basketball, so I joined them. I assumed my ride would be there by the time the center closed, so when the time came, I was sitting in the lobby and the janitor asked me if I had a ride. I told him my brother lived in town, but he stopped answering the phone, so my family had to come all the way from Springfield. He asked me how close they were, and I used the phone to call and see. When I told him where they were, he offered to meet them halfway at a gas station because he was going in that direction.

He was about seven-foot-tall and asked me if I wanted to go to college and play ball. He saw me play and he thought I was pretty good. I told him I wanted to go to North Carolina. He told me that's where he went to college, and he played against Michael Jordan and Larry Bird, and other big-name players. He asked me about my grades, and I told him I made good grades. We had a whole conversation with me making things up, all without him knowing that he had a fugitive in his car wanted for attempted murder. We got to the gas station and KeKe and her sister were in a white Cadillac. I got out the car, thanked him, and got in the car with them. The next day I was on the news. They said I picked the lock with a bobby pin and showed the false pin that I allegedly used and left in the backseat of the van. They also said they got an anonymous tip that I got in a white Cadillac. I never found out, but I always thought the tip came from the janitor.

I was staying in Nashville at KeKe's sister's house until her boyfriend said he didn't want me there anymore. I initially didn't want to call, but I called Cike and told him I needed to speak to him. I pulled up and there were a bunch of guys in the yard.

Cike walked up and said, "Man your brother ran off with some dope."

I immediately thought they were going to kill me.

"How much"

"A whole nine."
"Aw, I'm going to go get that and bring it back or bring the money back."

"Don't worry about it, I've already talked to your dad, and he's going to get it squared away. It's straight."

I was mad on the inside because I looked at Cike as a father figure because everything I had, had

come from him. Aside from that, I brought my
brother to him and introduced him, so him running
off looked bad on my behalf. He told me that I was
on the run and that I needed to get all of it behind
me. He said I needed to lay down and do the time
and get out and start a new life. He pulled out a bank
roll of money, gave me $500 and told me if I needed
anything, I could call him, but he wasn't going to give
me any dope. I went back and started plotting on how
to get some more money. KeKe's nephew was
reckless so I told hm about some people that I knew
from Springfield that had some money. He was down
to do whatever. We grab two other guys from
Nashville I didn't know, and we headed over to rob
the guy I was telling them about. They kicked the
door twice and it didn't open. They kicked the door
the third time and the door opened, and the guy was
inside having sex with his girlfriend. He jumped up
and grabbed the cover. I shot in the front door so he
couldn't see me because my face wasn't covered and
so he would have to duck his head and back up.
When he ducked, I slid into the kitchen and took my
shirt off to tie it around my face as a mask. I shot two

more times so he wouldn't see me come out the kitchen. I did a quick search in the living room and shot again into the room he was in so he would move out the way. I grabbed his pants, took the money out, about $1500, and I ran out leaving the other guys in there. They eventually called me trying to see what I took and where I was. I told them, "Fuck you, you shouldn't have even come with me, you don't even know me, you're lucky I didn't kill all ya'll and leave ya'll in there. Fuck ya'll, go back to Nashville." I hung up and they started texting me all the things they were going to do to me, but I kept it pushing. I called Kay and told her I needed a place to chill. She told me I could come to her house.

I still needed more money, so one of my classmates told me to take him with me whenever I had another lick. I already had one in mind. I told him the plan, and we went to hit the lick. We kicked the door in after the person left and searched two rooms. The guy I was with was trying to steal his shoes, so I knew he was a real rookie. I looked in the closet and found two pounds of weed on the floor. I pitched it to him and told him to hold it. After searching unsuccessfully, I stopped to think about where the money could possibly be. I started thinking about where I would hide my money. I patted the clothes down that were hanging in the closet, and I came to freshly dry-cleaned pair of pants. I felt the money in the pocket, took it out, and I pocketed the money. I told my classmate, "Come on, there's nothing in here."

We left and ran across the field to get back to the car. My classmate was heavier, so he was running behind me. I pulled the money out to count it and it was $10,000. I put the money back up and we got in the car. He asked me what we were going to do with the weed. I told him he could keep it because I didn't sell weed, it moved too slow for me. I told him to just give me something when he made something off it. He got excited, and we dropped him off. When he got out the car, I showed my cousin the money.

He said, "Damn cuz, how much is that?"

"Ten."

"Give me some."

I gave him $500.

I turned eighteen while I was on the run. I hired a lawyer for my attempted murder charge, and he told me he was going to turn me in January fifth. I decided I was going to have as much fun as I could. I met a girl who was going to Atlanta for New Year, so I went with her. Before I left, I put some dope in my cousin's car. I called him when he woke up to tell him what he needed to do with it. I used a rental that a junky rented out and gave him money and dope to extend the rental so I could drive myself and follow them to Atlanta. I didn't find out until later that he didn't extend the rental, but reported it stolen. When I got to Atlanta, I had a blast. They took me a club which was my first time. They took me to a restaurant named Houston's and that was my first experience eating filet mignon, and they also took me to a restaurant where they cooked the food in front of you.

I found out I had a cousin in town, so I called him to hang out. I passed Magic City riding around and remembered it was the strip club all the rappers talked about in their music. So, when I called my cousin to hang out, I invited him to go to Magic City with me. I had my brother's ID. When I walked in, I felt like a celebrity. We spent about two hours in the club, and we got private lap dances. When we left, my cousin went back to his house, and I went to spend the night with the girl I came with. We slept together that night with no protection.

I came back home January fourth. On January fifth my cousin was coming to get me, and when I came downstairs, I saw a detective on the right. I assumed he was there for me and knew who I was, so I took off running. When I ran, the detective drew his gun and told me to stop. The only reason I stopped was because I had a shoot to kill out on me because I was on the run for attempted murder. I put my hands in the air and he came to pat me down. He asked me who I was, and I kept telling him, he already knew who I was. He found my brother's ID and didn't recognize his name, so he told me he was going to run my name. He found car keys in my pocket and asked me if I knew whose keys they were, but I told him my cousin just asked me to follow him somewhere and those were the keys he gave me. The detective informed me that the car was reported stolen. The entire walk back to the car, I kept telling him he already knew who I was. He asked me who I was a final time, and I told him, "Joe Baker." He immediately got on the scanner and said he had me in custody and he needed a patrol car to escort me. They threw me in the car so fast that they never took my cell phone. I called my aunt and told them I was going to jail, and to call my lawyer because he didn't have to turn me in.

I assumed I was going back to juvenile, but since I turned eighteen while I was on the run, and they were charging me with theft for the stolen car, I was being charged as an adult. I sat in jail for the entire year, until November sixteenth. The case was resolved and closed, and I then went to court for the attempted murder case. They sent me back to juvenile. I got to a unit where there was a group of guys who were talking about escaping. This was my cup of tea. They talked about beating the staff up, going out the back door, and using tied up sheets to throw over the fence to escape. I decided I was going.

Within three days the escape plan took place. They came in the room to get me, but I had an idea to use this as a leverage to help me get out. While they were beating up the staff, I came out, and helped the staff members. If I didn't step in when I did, they would've immediately killed one of the staff members, but the staff member at least made it to the hospital before he died. I was the hero. I was able to use the phone when I wanted to, and I had clout.

The court tried to bound me over to an adult case, but I went to a preliminary hearing with my lawyer. He told me he could get me four years for the attempted murder by getting it down to aggravated assault, and one year for evading arrest when I took them on a high-speed chase. I accepted the five years. He told me I wasn't going back to juvenile because I was eighteen. He informed me they'd bound me over, I'd sit in jail for fourteen days, take a four-year probation, and be back at home. That's exactly what I did.

When I got back home, I went to stay with my momma. I got a job where my mom was working at a factory and I met a girl there and got her phone number. I wasn't there two weeks before I walked out on the job and left. I started working at IAC, another factory, and while I was working there, I hit another lick. A guy I grew up with wanted me to go with him because there was supposed to be a lot of pounds of weed, pills, and money. I told him I'd go. It got out that they were selling the weed from the lick, but I didn't go with them, so I called them. "Man, what's up I heard ya'll already hit the lick."

"Man, yea we already hit the lick."

"Well, what's up? I need some of that weed."

"We already sold everything, all of it is gone."

"What? So, ya'll went and hit the lick without me?"

"Yea man, everything's already gone."

"Man, pull up behind Pizza Hut, I want to holla at you." We both pulled up. I was in the car with one of my cousins. I wanted to look at him in his face, and I also wanted to see if they had some money on them. We talked passenger window to driver window.

"Man, why ya'll did that?"

"Ma, we just went and did it. Next time you can go with us."

"Man, listen. If anybody is going to be doing the robbing in this town, it's going to be me. If you're going without me, you owe me a cut. You have thirty minutes to go get the weed, and if you don't come back with it, I'm shooting your momma's house up." I looked at the guy he had with him and said, "And I'm shooting your granny's house up. Go get me some of that weed or it's going to be some problems." I rolled up the window and pulled off. They called my phone telling me I was tripping, but I told them I wasn't, and I was dead serious. While we were talking, we ended up behind them in traffic somehow. I cocked the gun in the phone and asked if he could hear it. He told me he could, so I told him to look behind him. I took the gun and held it outside the car pointing it at his car and told him I wasn't playing. Ironically, I told them to get the weed and bring it to my mom's house.

We pulled up at my mom's house and waited. They called and said they had the weed, so I told them to pull in my mom's driveway backwards. They backed in. I told them to roll the window down, throw the weed out, and pull off. They did what I told them. I got out to get the weed and it was four pounds. I made about $1500-$1600.

While I was at work and I was sitting down reading a book. A woman walked over to me.

"I just had to walk all the way over here to see if you were really doing what I thought you were doing. You're not a regular street nigga. I heard a lot about you, but when I saw you reading that book, I thought there was something about you. You have a calling on your life. You want something to drink? I'm going to the breakroom to get something to drink."

I pulled a lot of money out of my pocket.

She said, "Boy, if you don't put that up. You can't be walking around with that kind of money; these people will think you don't even need a job out here."

I brushed it off. Two days later I quit my job and got back in the streets. I was getting dope from one of my aunties. A guy named JR reached out and said he wanted to do business with me. He wanted to sell me his overages for a really cheap price. I did business for a while until one day I stopped answering the phone and kept his money. I was cooking my own dope, so someone else came to me and asked me to cook his dope. I told him I would so long as I kept the overages. He agreed and asked me to sell his dope too. I asked him how much he wanted, and he told me $1400. I agreed, but I also kept his money. I had in my mind to get back to where I was financially by any means necessary. I didn't care who was in my way.

I was riding with Peanut one day, when the guy whose $1400 I kept, pulled up beside us. He kept telling me to roll my window down, and I kept pointing to my ear trying to sign that I couldn't hear him. He motioned for me to roll my window down, but I kept pointing to my ear. When the light turned green, I told Peanut to pull off. He called me and I sent him to voicemail.

He left me a message, "Jackboy, Jackboy, what you gonna do? What you gonna do when they come for you?"

I called him back and told him if he ever left a voicemail on my phone like that again, it was going to be problems. I didn't hear from him for a while, until one of my friends went to the club, and came back and told me the guy told him he needed to stop messing with me and mess with him. He told him I was out here robbing everybody, and we couldn't get money like that. I was sitting on the porch swing at my mom's house when I saw him pull up to the gas station. I ran inside and got my gun and went across the street.

When he saw me he said, "What's up?"

By the time I got to the car, he was back in the car with a car full of people. I stuck my head in window and told him, "Listen here. If I ever hear you've been telling my people not to mess with me because I'm robbing people, I'm going to come see about you and it's going to be problems."

"Man, lil Boo, you be tripping."

"Nah, I ain't tripping, I'm out here getting it how I live and it ain't gon be no issues about me." I told all the people in the car they needed to stop messing with him, and mess with me. They all fell out laughing.

I ended up moving to Clarksville from Springfield to be with this girl named Tasha. While living in Clarksville with her, I was still selling dope. I actually wanted to be with this girl, so I wanted to get out and get a job. I wanted to get out of the streets before I ended up getting in some trouble. I had about three grams of dope left. My cousin got out of prison and flagged me down one day. I had about $1200 sitting in my lap. When I stopped, he reached in and jokingly grabbed my money. I told him not to play with me like that, and not to ever touch my money. In spite of that, we started hanging out after that.

We were riding around one day and stopped at his house. I saw where he kept his stash of money and weed. We went to a basketball game later that night. I was telling him how I was going to get out of the game and I only had three grams left. I came up with a plan to leave the game at half time and go rob his house and come back to the game. Terrell came and got me, we kicked the door in, ransacked the place, robbed him, he brought me back to the game, and I gave my cousin the dope for free. We left and my cousin went home. When he got home, he called me telling me to come over because someone broke in his house.

I pulled up to his house. I looked at the mess I made and told him not to worry about it because we would find out who did it and take care of it. He assumed it was a guy he was beefing with because they were messing with the same girl. He never found out it was really me. I did it because he disrespected

148

me by touching my money that day. I hit one more lick for four pounds of weed before getting out of the game. I split the weed with Peanut, and we got $1000 a piece. I went back to Clarksville to get a job. Tasha went with me to the interview, and they told me I got the job and when I could start. Tasha gave me head while I was driving for getting the job, and that was the first time I got head while driving. She told me she was proud of me.

A few day later, my friend from Springfield named Tony got into with someone and tried to shoot him. The bullet ricocheted off the ground and hit a girl in the neck. He called me needing a place to stay. I told him he could come stay at my Tasha's house, so I met him halfway and brought him to Clarksville. He started selling dope off my porch in the projects. When he ran out, he asked me for work, but I told him I was through, and I was going to work my job. He then asked me to hit a lick with him. I didn't want to deny him because he was my friend and he was in a bind. I called Peanut and asked him to connect us to a lick. We left Clarksville to head to Springfield. On the way there we passed through

Cooper Town. Everyone knows to do the speed limit in this city. Everyone would always say, "The Cooper troopers be through there." Riding through, I had a gun in the car and no license, and Tony was on the run. A police car got behind us and turned their lights on. I looked at Tony and asked him what he wanted me to do: Pull over or take off? He told me to just pull over. As I was pulling over, the police flew right past us. We decided to keep going to Springfield to hit the lick.

We got prepared to hit the lick, and the plan was to follow the guy home and rob him. We didn't know exactly where he lived so we couldn't do the usual kicking the door in and ransacking the place. The guy was under the tree, a spot in the projects where people sold drugs, and we knew that if we robbed him there, we wouldn't have everything. After waiting some time, and the guy not leaving, we decided to change the plan and kidnap him to make him take us to his house so we could steal everything. Terrell, Peanut, Tony and I approached him. We had an AK47 and a 9mm and we pointed it at him and told him to get in the car. We took his keys and let

Terrell out on the next street over to take the guy's car and follow us to his house. We threw him in the backseat and Tony was in the back pistol whipping him. I turned around to see what was going on, and he let off two shots in Tasha's car. We thought he shot him, but he was just letting the gun off in front of his face trying to scare him. Peanut and I looked at each other in agreement that Tony was tripping.

When we got to his house, the guy was bleeding from being whipped all the way there. Peanut and I got out, and Tony got out with the guy we were robbing. He told him to take us inside. The guy said his kids were in there and he wasn't letting us in his house. He said he'd go in and get everything and bring it back out. Tony looked at him like he was crazy, and they proceeded to go back and forth. While they were arguing, Terrell pulled up behind us in the guy's car. Terrell got out with the keys. I took the keys from him and set them on the trunk so the guy could take us in there. The guy took the keys and turned to walk off like he was going to do what he said, and not what we instructed him. Tony grabbed his shoulder, turned him around, and shot him in the torso. Terrell took off. Peanut, Tony and I jumped back in the car. The guy fell to the ground and was crawling towards the door. We pulled off and dropped the guns off in a car my mom didn't use anymore that was at her house and headed back to Clarksville.

We cleaned the blood out the car the best we could when we got back. I laid in the bed that night with Tasha, and she kept asking me what was wrong. I denied anything was wrong until she turned over and went to sleep. I was worried about what happened. I eventually went to sleep, but it wasn't a deep sleep because I heard Tony pass in the hallway and say he didn't kill anybody. I jumped out the bed and ran downstairs and asked Peanut what was going on. He told me the guy we tried to rob was dead. I told them they had to leave.

I took Tony to the mall and he had someone come and get him. I took Peanut back to Springfield and on the way there, a detective called me. He told me he needed me to come in for questioning because my name came up in a murder that took place the night before. I told him I didn't know anything, and if

I wasn't under arrest then I wasn't coming in for questioning. When we hung up, he called Peanut's phone. Peanut said the same thing and got off the phone with him. My mom called me and asked me what happened last night and wanted to know whose blood was on the gun. She went to the car and found the guns. I told her I'd talk to her about it when I got there. I dropped Peanut off at his house, but I didn't know my mom was there. I headed to my mom's house, but before I got there, she called me and told me Peanut's mom was going to take him down to the police department because the police called her and told her he had something to do with the murder. I told her she didn't need to do that, but she did it anyways. Peanut spent three hours talking to the detective.

When they finally came back, the first thing I asked him was, "What did you tell them?"

His mom interjected, "All ya'll going to jail! All ya'll did that shit!"

I looked at her and told her, "I didn't do a mutha fucking thing." I told Peanut, "Let's go to the store real quick."

His mom interjected again, "No, he's not going nowhere with you."

I looked at Peanut and told him again, "Come on, let's walk to the store real quick." We headed towards the store. I asked him again, "Man, what did you tell those folks?"

"Man, I put it all on Tony. I told them I didn't know what was going on, he said he wanted to go pick up some dope, and he ended up doing all that. I told them I was scared for my life which is why I didn't want to come in and talk."

"And you didn't get arrested or get a charge or anything?"

"I told them I'd be a witness in the case."

I believed him because he went down there and incriminated himself by telling them he was at the murder scene, so I thought he didn't tell them about me. We left it at that, and he left with his mom. I went to a lawyer to get me on at job corps so I could get out of town. He told me filed the paperwork to get me in front of a judge because it took a judge's consent since I was on probation. While all this is happening, Peanut started messing with KeKe, and every time I called him, he didn't answer the phone. I drove up KeKe's street and saw him sitting on the porch.

KeKe yelled, "He ain't going nowhere with you, you going to jail, I hope they give you the mutha fuckin electric chair! I'ma make sure he go to court on you and tell it all!"

I was confused. Peanut didn't say anything. I asked him, "Man, what's up?"

He told me, "Man don't even worry about her, we can't be seen together, which is why I stopped answering the phone. Don't worry about it, we're going to be straight."

"Man, we don't even have a story together, what you mean we straight? And you didn't even say nothing to her about what she said!"

"Man, you know she crazy, don't worry about her."

I pulled off and left. A couple days later, I called Peanut to no avail. My court date was the next day, so as I sat in my room at my mom's house, she knocked on the door and pointed to the phone quietly telling me the police were on the phone. Since I was familiar with how they operated, I looked out the window to see if they were sitting outside, and they were parked at the gas station across the street. I picked up the phone to buy me time to put my shoes on. I walked out the door to see if there were other officers outside, but there weren't. He told me I needed to come in so they could talk to me about the case, but I told them if I wasn't under arrest, I wasn't going. I hung up and got on the phone with Terrell. He told me I needed to go talk to them because they just left his house and were coming to arrest me. By the time we got off the phone, not even fifteen seconds later, a police officer came through the front, and another through the back. They pulled me out my room, put me on the ground, cuffed me and read me my rights. I was being arrested for first degree premeditated murder, special aggravated kidnapping, special aggravated robbery, and three counts of felony murder.

My mom started crying, and my sister ran in the back. They picked me up, took me outside, and placed me in a patrol car. They took me down to the police department instead of taking me straight to jail. They put me in a room and start interrogating me, asking me what happened. I started lying and giving fake alibis. They told me they knew I was lying, that they were going to get Tasha's car and take pictures of the car, and that Peanut came down and gave a statement. They read and showed me his signed statement. They showed Terrell's statement, but I didn't read it. They told me they both didn't have a reason to incriminate themselves and that they knew their statements were true. The whole thing was now on me and Tony. I realized I had a lawyer and told them to call my lawyer. They called my lawyer, put him on speaker and he told me he would be there shortly. He advised me to make a statement because if I didn't, I would go down for the murder because Tony was going to make a statement.

When he said that, I started making statements. They wouldn't accept any statement unless it fully involved myself and incriminated me. I finally made a statement they accepted, and I signed the statement, and they took me to jail. They sat me in the same unit as Tony who was now my charge partner. Tony was being charged for voluntary man slaughter. My cell mate told me the whole story of exactly what happened with our case. He told me that Tony was down there telling everybody that I was the one who did the shooting. There was no way he could've known the story unless Tony was really telling people that, so I knew he was telling the truth.

I was in my cell that night and I couldn't sleep. I was thinking about my kid, my family, my freedom, everything. I was thinking I was going to sit in prison for the rest of my life because this was a murder case and wasn't like the petty cases I had beforehand. I decided I was going to play crazy again because I thought it helped me out last time, although in reality it didn't. They let us out for rec the next day and I refused to go back in after rec. They wrestled me and threw me down and started choking me.

There were about six officers and they couldn't get me in the cell, so they called the captain of the jail. The captain was my cousin, so he calmed me down and talked to me and asked me what I wanted. I told him I wanted to be moved to another unit because I didn't want to be where my Tony was, especially with him telling the case. I knew the District Attorney could talk to my cell mate and it would seem like I was the one who told him everything and paint me guilty.

They moved me downstairs where it was really quiet, and I had too much time to think. A part of me really was suicidal, but another part of me wanted to get out of jail. I had a razor, so when they came to check on me, I told them to call the sergeant and if he didn't, I was going to kill myself. He immediately called and said he had a suicide threat and they needed to come downstairs. Three or four officers came down and told me to put the razor down because that was the only way they could come in the cell. I refused, and when I saw that the sergeant still didn't come, I said, "So, ya'll think I'm playing huh?" I slit my wrist right then one time. My flesh opened like a fish and there was a lot of blood. It scared me and excited me at the same time. They decided to open the door, and by that time I cut myself two more times. They rushed me, grabbed me, and slammed me down. They covered my wrist to try and stop the bleeding. They called the ambulance and rushed me to the hospital. They hospital gave me stitches and sent me back to the jail.

They had me in a suicide cell under observation. They called Mobile Crisis and after their evaluation, they told me I was faking. I would flood my cell all the time, argue and cuss the officers out trying to act like I was crazy. I came up with the idea that I wanted to bite the stitches out of my hand. I bit the stitches out and I popped my wrist to open the wound back up so it would bleed again. As I was bleeding, the officers stood outside the cell looking at me like I was crazy. They told me they were instructed by the captain not to call the ambulance anymore because I was faking. I asked them, "So, ya'll are just going to let me die?"

They told me, "The sergeant told us not to call the ambulance anymore and the medic is out for the rest of the day, so we don't know what you're going to do."

I just stood there bleeding. One of the officers came and said he could stitch me up. They advised him against it because he wasn't certified to do so. He looked at me and asked me if I wanted him to stitch me up. I told him, "If you know how to do it, then yea, you gon have to, cause clearly they're not calling the ambulance." They cuffed me and took me to the medic room. The officer got all the stuff out and stitched me up. He told me that he went to school for it briefly, but it wasn't his field. He asked me not to say anything that could get him fired because he just wanted to help me. I agreed and told him he had nothing to worry about. They put me back in the observation cell.

Where the cell was located, was right in the vicinity of where people made bond. I could see the door that people walked out to leave, and I could see the buttons they pushed. I also heard the doors unlock when they pushed the buttons. I was getting in so much trouble that the sergeant would just take me out my cell to clean up. One night I was cleaning up and the officer told me she had to put me back in my cell because they were going to book somebody. She told me that she'd let me back out once they got him booked and processed. She put me back in my cell and pushed the door up, but she didn't lock it. I turned the light off in my cell and laid down to see if I could go the rest of the night without them knowing the door was unlocked. I was going to try to escape on the next shift because they wouldn't know my door was unlocked either. The lady came around with my meds and tried to unlock the door, and realized the door was already unlocked. She went crazy announcing that the door was left unlocked and that it should never be left unlocked. She blew my chance.

A few days later I got angry about something, so I flooded the cell. Ten to fifteen minutes passed before they even knew I flooded it. Water was everywhere in intake. The officers got so mad they came to my cell and tried to beat me up. I slammed one officer on the ground because he slipped. While I was reaching to grab the other officer, my cousin the sergeant was coming into the intake area where we were. He yelled out for us to stop. The officer that I slammed to the ground was getting up and cocked his fist back to punch me.

My cousin said, "If you hit him, I'll fire you right here on the spot."

The officer stopped and my cousin looked at me standing with one cuff on and asked me, "Man, what is wrong with you?"

I told him, "I want to get out of here." My cousin walked me out of the cell into intake and sat me down. He was talking to me trying to calm me down. I looked at him and asked, "Why won't you get me transferred?"

"Trust me, I'm trying to get you transferred. I don't want you in my jail. You need to get from round here. You cause too many problems, every day."

"What you think I'm trying to do run or something? They told me you instructed them not to call the ambulance the other day."

"I didn't tell them anything."

"You think I'm trying to run, don't you?"

He said, "I don't know, are you?"

I looked at him and said, "You think this place can hold me?"

"I don't know, can it?"

I told him, "Man, your staff been trying to let me go, and the next time they do it, I'm walking straight out of here."

"The night they do is the night I fire every one of them."

The next day the lady officer did the same thing she previously did. When she let me out to clean, someone was coming in to get booked. She told me she'd let me out after they got him booked and put me in the cell and closed the door without locking it. I cut the light off and laid down. The other lady came through with the medication. I jumped up and told her I didn't want the medication and I was fine. She had me sign a refusal paper and went back down the hall. The lady forgot she left my cell unlocked like last time. I laid there like I was sleep until third shift came in.

I laid there for about two hours before somebody else came into intake.

He said, "I'm making bond! Don't even put me in no holding cell, I'm making bond! My family already here, they followed the police car up here!"

I got up to see if it was someone I knew so I could tell them to move out the way when they buzz him out, so I could run out.

I didn't know him, but I heard the officer say, "His family is already here. Do you want me to buzz them in?"

The other officer said, "Yea, you can go ahead and buzz him in."

The officer looked at me standing in the door and waved. I nodded my head. I stood there waiting on the woman to hit certain buttons, and she hit both buttons. I heard two clicks that let me know both doors were unlocked. I push the door open and the officer turned around and looked at me. It was like everything was in slow motion. I look at the guy and I read his lips say, "What the fuck." Before the officer could really understand what was going on, I was gone. I ran through the first door, and the guy being booked had family coming in, so I pushed her out the way. she screamed as I pushed through the second door. When I pushed through the second door, I was outside.

I took off running downhill and I was running so fast I started tumbling. I tumbled to the bottom and by that time an officer was chasing me. He yelled out pleading for me not to run because I was only going to make it worse for myself. I bounced up like a rubber ball and ran across the street. I didn't run far because I knew police would be out looking for me. I checked every car door in the vicinity. There was a guy who was a couple grades ahead of me in school who lived nearby. I checked his car door and it was unlocked. I laid down in the front of his car for three or four hours. I heard police cars passing by all night. I knew I got away, but I was too scared to raise up because I thought it would be just my luck for me to raise up and the police would be sitting right in front of the car.

I mustered up enough courage to raise up and look. There weren't any police. I got out and ran to DLo's house nearby. I knew where they kept the key to get in the back door, so I let myself in. I took a shower, brushed my teeth, and put DLo's clothes on. I laid in his bed thinking about what I was going to do. DLo's house was like one house separated into two units. I went outside and walked to the front part of the house to act like I wasn't already in the house. I knocked on the DLo's little brother's window and somebody looked out. I motioned for them to come downstairs. I went back downstairs and waited but he never came. I did it a second time, and he never came. I went to the front door and knocked. I heard DLo's dad ask who I was, so I told him it was me. He told me he didn't know how I got there but I couldn't stay. He was already on probation and police already came looking for me and asking questions. I asked him where DLo was because I was knocking on the window looking for him. Apparently, it was Johnny, the girl I was messing with whose house DLo used to drop me off at, who was looking out the window, not DLo's little brother. Johnny was dating DLo's little brother at the time. I said, "Well, somebody give me a ride then."

DLo's dad said, "Ain't nobody in here giving you no ride either."

Johnny spoke up and volunteered to take me. She took me to Jeff's house. I told her to call Terrell because I needed a ride to Clarksville. I told her not to tell him I was there. I didn't know at the time that Terrell's statement was against me, I just thought he covered himself. So, when he got there and saw me come out the back room, he jumped as if I scared him. I thought he was surprised to see me out of jail, but in retrospect he was scared because he thought I was going to do something to him because of his statement. Terrell and another female cousin took me to Clarksville and dropped me off at a girl's house who said I could stay with her. I told them I made bond, not that I broke out of jail.

Her brother came and asked me how I got out of jail because he heard my bond was half a million dollars. I told him I had a bond reduction hearing and I made bond. He took me at my word and went in the kitchen to cook something to eat. While he was cooking, he was watching TV, and the news came on. I came on the news, so he froze the TV and called me in the kitchen.

He told me, "You didn't have to lie to me, you could've told me you escaped from jail."

I told him I didn't want to get them in trouble by involving them. They let me stay anyways, so I went in the room and laid down to go to sleep. While I was sleeping someone shook me and told me the police had the house surrounded. I heard them come over the bullhorn.

"Joe Baker we know you're in the house! We don't want you or anyone else to get hurt so come outside unarmed with your hands up!"

I still thought I could escape so I go to the window and put my hands underneath the blinds so they could see my hands. I put my head underneath the blinds so I could see exactly where the police were so I could make a run for it. When they said they had the house surrounded, they meant that. There were police, marshals, ambulances, Mobile Crisis, a helicopter hovering the premises, police behind trees, and bushes. Police were everywhere. It looked like a scene out of a movie. They announced over the bullhorn they were calling the house phone, so I answered the phone. The lieutenant in charge of the operation was on the line and he tried to talk me into coming out. I told him I wasn't coming out and I had a knife in my hand. I told him if his officers came in, they'd have to kill me. He told me he would hate for it to happen that way, but if they came in and I had a weapon in my hand, they would shoot to kill. I told him that was better than going to jail.

I called Tasha and told her I was going to let them kill me. She told me I was selfish and not to do it. I hung up with her, and the lieutenant called me on three-way with Tasha. I guess the phone was tapped.

They both tried to convince me to go outside. I told them before I came out, I wanted something to drink. I only said that so I could look in the back of the house and see how many officers were outside. They could see me as I walked to the refrigerator and opened the door. The lieutenant told me to turn and look out the window and I would see him standing there. I got a root beer, closed the fridge, and looked out the window. The officer waved at me and I waved back. I walked back into the living room and I knew there was no way out and I was going to jail.

I knew their mom took Seroquel, so I went in their mom's room and took some. After I took it, I went outside to surrender, and they arrested me. Reporters from every station were outside asking me how I escaped. I told them all that they let me out. They took me to jail and by the time I got there I was feeling the effects of the Seroquel. We walked in the jail and they tried to fingerprint me, but it was as if I was out of my body. They kept asking me if I had taken anything, but I stood there with no response at all. They rushed me upstairs to the medic. He asked me if I had taken anything and I knew at that point I

171

had to say yes. I shook my head yes and he asked what I took. I shrugged my shoulders to signal I didn't know. He gave me a small cup of brown liquid and told me to take it, and I would throw up in ten seconds. Not even five seconds later, I threw up everything that was in my stomach. Five minutes later I was feeling back to normal.

Two TBI (TN Bureau of Investigation) officers came in my cell, "You know what we're here for right?"

I responded, "Yea."

"Well how did you get out?"

"Is anyone else getting in trouble for this besides me?"

They both said, "Nope."

"Well I don't have anything to say if I'm the only one going down for it." They left my cell and transferred me to Nashville to a maximum-security prison for safe keeping until my case was over. I went through intake and they gave me an all-white jump suit with a blue stripe down the middle. I thought they were taking me to maximum security, but they took me to 7C where they take all the mental health patients. They walked me in like I was a mass murderer. I had fifteen officers around me as I walked in handcuffs and shackles. When I walked in people were kicking the door, and screaming, and others were standing in the door looking crazy. They took me in my cell and slammed the door. I wasn't in my cell thirty minutes before I popped the water sprinkler. They came to the door and told me they were going to leave me in there until the water stopped. They meant that. I stayed in there with the water running for about thirty minutes. I knew then that these weren't the people to be playing with. When the water stopped, they took me to a different cell and cleaned up the water. This cell had a camera and no water sprinkler. I sat there for two weeks with no shower. The only thing I was allowed to do was eat. They broke me that quick. I knew I had to act right.

When they finally let me go outside, I met a guy everyone called Slim.

He asked me, "When did you get here? I never saw you before."

I told him, "I got here a couple weeks ago but they had me in the observation cell because I popped the water sprinkler when I first got here."

"Oh, that was you who popped the water sprinkler? They kept you in there the whole time, didn't they?"

I told him they did. He then asked me what I was in for and I told him I was in for safe keeping because I escaped from the county jail.

He said, "Oh, you're the one the officers have been talking about. I saw the newspaper clipping on you. You have a charge partner, don't you?"

"Yea."

"You better tell on him."

Confused I said, "Huh?"

"You better tell on him. I know you probably one of those dudes who believe in street codes and how it's supposed to go, but you better tell on him."

"Man, I ain't finna do that."

He came to the fence and said, "Listen to me youngblood. This week I've been here going on thirty years. I've slept with men, lost my momma, lost my daddy, and no kids. I've only got one person who writes me that I found on the chat line years ago. I lost my whole life in here man. I've been to maximum security a couple times, been stabbed a couple times, stabbed a few people, been in all kinds of fights and gang fights. I've fought with the police, beat up the police, been jumped on by the police, and I'm innocent. So, if you're innocent or can tell the truth about your case... listen to me. Tell the truth and go home."

The only thing I heard him say was he was sleeping with men. He walked off and kept on walking and talking as if he didn't just tell me everything he said.

I went back in and had to see the psychiatrist because I was still playing the crazy role. They gave me some medication called Haldol. While I was doing pushups, my whole body stopped, and my leg started lifting off the ground by itself. I screamed for help and told them my body locked up and I couldn't move. They came in and gave me a shot in my butt and told me they weren't supposed to give me Haldol medicine without Cogentin. I refused to take that medicine again, so they switched my medication to Seroquel, and they finally moved me upstairs out of the mental health unit into the maximum-security unit. When I got upstairs, Slim was there. I was back and forth to court, and there were a bunch of guys who had been locked up a long time so as I was telling them my case, they told me what motions to file, what I needed to do, how I needed to do it, and to fire my lawyer. They became certified paralegals and I listened to them thinking I was getting the best legal advice. In my cell I watched Boston Legal and I thought I was Danny Crane. I thought I knew everything about the law.

When I was getting ready for court one day, a lady came to my cell to tell me to pack up because I was going to court in the morning. I tried to talk to her when I first arrived. She asked me if I was getting out, and I told her I was. I jokingly asked her if she'd let me call her when I got home. She brushed me off, but when she walked off, she wrote her name and number down and slid it under my door and winked at me. When she walked off, I thought to myself, "I'm not going home, I'll be right back." When I went to court, they put my court date off again. I came back and the lady was working third shift that night. She came to my cell to talk to me as I was watching a show called Monk. I jokingly told her to come in my cell.

She looked at me and said, "You trying to get you some ain't you?"

I told her yes, but I was just joking and didn't think she was going to take me seriously. She took her keys out and stuck them in the door so she could come in and I stopped her. I told her, "Hold on!"

She replied, "You said you wanted me to come in."

I told her to let me finish watching my show, but I said that because I was scared. I told her my show was going to end in the next fifteen minutes and she told me she would come back. While she was gone, I wiped my cell down and moved things around, thinking I was going to make it smell good for her. In my mind, I was thinking, "She's going to come in my cell for real." Fifteen minutes pass and she came to the door. When she came in, I stepped to the back of the cell thinking she was trying to get me in trouble. I also had a thought that I could scream rape and get out of my case, but I didn't. When she stepped all the way in, she closed the door behind her.

She pulled her pants down and said, "You ain't trying to do nothing for real."

She laid down on my mat, so I went inside of her with no protection and when I finished, I ejaculated in her. She got up and left, I guess to go clean up. I cleaned up myself and as I was pacing the floor, all I could think about was how I couldn't wait to tell everybody the next day what happened. I thought I was a king because I was getting some in prison. After she cleaned up, she came back to the cell and told me to give her about an hour and she'd come back in, and we'd do everything. She told me we'd get naked and do it all, but I told her she didn't have to come back. I told her to catch me another time because I didn't want to do it anymore.

I went outside the next day and told everybody on the yard. A couple days later she came to my cell.

She asked me, "What are you trying to do? Get me fired?"

I played dumb. "What are you talking about?"

"Everywhere I go somebody is telling me how I messed around with you. Who did you tell?"

"I didn't tell anybody."

"Well, you had to tell somebody because I know I didn't tell anybody to get myself fired." As she walked off, she said, "I ain't fooling with you no more."

I blew my chance with her because she never slept with me again after that.

I stayed there a year going back and forth to court with them putting my court date off. I went through three or four lawyers. Whenever I told a lawyer that in my statement, I told the detectives I wanted to call my attorney and I never should have been questioned afterwards, they didn't believe me, so I fired them.

At some point they moved me to a different jail that didn't have maximum security and they assigned me a caseworker. My caseworker was a woman who came to see me once a week. I noticed that she began to take a liking to me. In the middle of one of my sessions one day I asked her, "You like me, don't you?" As I said that, I reached and grabbed her hands, and she let me hold her hands.

She said, "What? Why would you say that?"

We sat and talked, and she never answered me, but I knew she did. She started coming to see me twice a week. One day she came to see me to tell me that if I didn't see her anymore after that day, that she'd always stay in touch with me. They had her under investigation assuming she was bringing me stuff in. They thought we were sleeping together because when we went in our visitation room, we'd always close the door. We never slept together, but she ended up losing her job and I didn't see her anymore.

A big flood hit Nashville and they had to move to a different jail again. I hated it there. Their commissary and food weren't good, and I couldn't get a good reception on my TV. I started playing suicidal and they moved me to a suicide cell, stripped me naked, and put me in a paper suit. This was a method they used to try to break you so you wouldn't do it again. In the cell there was no mat, so I had to sleep on concrete in the cold. I stayed there for three days until my court date.

I got a lawyer that not only believed that I shouldn't have been questioned, but she investigated it. I was supposed to go straight to the jail, and I was never supposed to be questioned at the police station, especially for the four hours they kept me there. My lawyer spoke with the District Attorney and the District Attorney offered me twelve years. I declined and asked for eight. He said he would split the difference and offer me ten. We then moved on to the escape charge. Since I sat in jail for a year waiting for this court date, I tried to get time served, but they refused. We went to trial on the escape, and I was found guilty. The sentence only carried one to two years, so the District Attorney offered one year before the judge sentenced me, so I accepted.

I was now charged with attempt to commit special aggravated robbery, which they made up because it didn't exist, but it was a drop down from murder. I was also charged with a felony escape charge. This gave me an eleven-year sentence at thirty percent meaning I was eligible to see the parole board after thirty percent of my time was served. After returning to the jail I escaped from because no other jails would accept me due to no longer being in safe keeping status, I spent three days in the cell with someone I knew before they transported me off to my first prison.

Chapter 7: The Transition

When I got to the prison, I had to go through classification which was a point system that determined your security level, from minimum security to maximum security. I was there for two weeks and I found out my uncle, my dad's brother, was there who used to be a big-time gang member. I used to send him dope to the prison while I was in the streets. I heard he changed his life and gave his life to Christ and was doing much better. I wanted to use that to my advantage, so I sent him a letter and let him know I was there, and I wanted to stay. He was going to see what he could do about keeping me there. I wanted to stay there, get around my uncle, stay out the way, do my time, and get back home. After classification, it was determined that I couldn't stay because my points were so high, partly because of my escape charge. I had to go to close security. That meant I was being sent to one of the worst prisons in the state that I heard was called the Thunder Dome.

The night before, they informed us we were leaving in the morning. My celly, which is my cell mate, and I decided to rob people of their commissary so we would have some when we got to the next prison. During recreational times we could roam the pod, so used that time to go in our neighbor's cells and take their commissary. In the morning, I got to the next prison. We were all on lockdown because someone on close security got out for rec and beat up and stabbed an officer. I couldn't call home for three days. I was put in a two-man cell with an affiliated rolling sixty Crip who cooked liquor, kept knives in the cell, and got to use a cell phone all the time. He let me call home so long as I put some minutes on it. I called home and got a minute card from one of my friends and told everyone where I was. My dad was in another prison and he had a cell phone too. I got in touch with him and he already knew where I was. He asked me if I wanted to come where he was because he knew the warden well and could make a phone call to get me there. I had to stay at the prison I was already at for six months and while I was there, I got my first job in the kitchen. This was a good job because I was able to take back food, and I always got to make money because when people wanted extra food, they'd pay me in commissary for it.

My first few weeks there were good. I found out KeKe's nephew was there with a life sentence for murder. When her nephew found out I was there he tried to get me in the cell with him by putting in a cell change request. That lead me to getting in an altercation with my current cell mate because he felt as if I should've told him first, so he could get his preferred celly in the cell with him instead of allowing administration to place a random person. I believe he was only mad because he got attached to me in part because I was a good celly. I was clean, we got along, and I always had extra food. I switched cells anyway to the cell with KeKe's nephew. While I was in the kitchen, people always wanted to transfer weed and narcotics to the hole through those of us that worked in the kitchen because we were allowed outside of the cell. Having this job allowed me to move around during lockdowns when other people couldn't.

One day some Kitchen Crips paid me to take some weed over to someone in the hole. I took the $100 worth of weed and accidentally gave it to the wrong person. They later came to my cell and told me I had to not only pay back the $100, but I had to pay an additional $100. I refused to pay, and KeKe's nephew told them I refused to pay. They told me when the doors popped, we were going to "fall in." This meant we were going to fight. Before it could happen, officers came by giving everyone who was leaving their bags so they could pack, and they gave me and KeKe's nephew a bag. I was being transferred to the prison my dad was at, and he was going to court. When they found out I was leaving they told me wherever I was at, I would still have to pay the Kitchen Crips at the next prison. I didn't pay it any mind. While I was leaving, a Kitchen Crip was out of his cell cleaning up. I saw them pass him a knife under the door. They made a call to stick on me, meaning stab me, before I left, since he was the one out of his cell. He couldn't get close to those of us coming out, and he stood and stared at me telling me I was lucky. I got on the bus and left.

When I got to the prison with my dad, I was still on close security. I sent word out to him to let him know I was there. They sent commissary back and asked me if I needed anything. The first thing I thought was I wanted a cell phone, so they sent one over. I was placed in a one-man cell because I still had a few months left on close security. I slept all day and stayed up all night calling everybody. I took my one hour of rec daily, and took my showers every Monday, Wednesday, and Friday. I had a TV and a cell phone, so I was comfortable. My dad tried to get me moved out of close security early but the only way they would shorten my six-month sentence was if I took an anger management class. They told me this class would knock days off my sentence, so I took the class and got out a month early. My brother was also in the same prison for a drug charge, so my dad was trying to get him moved to where we were too. A few days before I was getting out of close security and moved to compound, my dad and his friend were busted with cell phones, heroine, and tobacco. They were running an operation getting it through the mail.

So, as they sent me to compound, my dad got sent to close security. We switched places.

Tony was also at the prison. I was concerned about this because I knew I made a statement, and he could easily use it against me by accusing me of being a snitch. I didn't think he would because we grew up together, but there was no way for me to really know. I was across from Tony and we were waiting on my brother to be moved. During rec one day, I was talking to one of my dad's friends.

He asked me my name and when he found out, he said, "Oh, you're Joe Baker's son? What gang are you?"

This was the first question everybody asked you upon introduction. I explained if anything I was Folk, but I hadn't gone through the initiation. I got introduced to a lot of the G's and everyone knew my dad, so I was automatically accepted, and everyone wanted me to be GD. My dad finally got out of the hole and was transferred back to the unit where I was. I let him use my cell phone so he could get things in order. He was still trying to figure out a way to keep the operation running.

This was my first time being around my dad outside of visitation. It was different. He was locked up my entire life and now I was standing in the same cell as him. I was looking at the things he collected over the years; an old boombox, old TV, old typewriter. I could tell just by looking at his things that he had been gone for a long time unlike someone like me who had a flat screen TV, and a handheld radio. His clothes even looked different. We talked and cooked a meal. Every meal was mixed with noodles. We cut up a summer sausage, with tuna, chicken, and mixed it all together. We added cheese and got some tortilla shells and made burritos.

The night my dad got out of close security, I sat there thinking about my entire life, everything I had done, where I was in jail at that moment, my dad being in the cell across from me, Tony in the other cell, and my cousin which was my dad's sister's son, in a cell down the hall. It was like a family reunion in there. A few days later my dad was reclassified and was going to be moved to another prison. This hurt me because I was just beginning to get close to him. While we were waiting for him to be moved my brother finally got moved into our area. Everyday my brother, my dad and I met at the place my dad worked and talked and hung out.

I was upset thinking over everything, and I was trying to figure out a way to get everything out I was feeling about all the time my dad missed. He was the one who gave my brother and I our dope plugs, we were in prison, and he was the reason we both got affiliated with Folk gang. I felt like he contributed to all of it and he was the main reason we were in prison. We were sitting talking about my dad's girlfriend because Christmas was coming up. I told him my daughter, which was his grandchild, wanted a laptop for Christmas that was $250. I asked him to pay for half and I would pay for the other half. He told me to wait until he knew how much money he had left because his girlfriend's daughter wanted something for Christmas as well.

I said, "What?"

He responded, "Just hold up til I know what my money's looking like cause I want to be able to get everybody something."

"Fuck her!"

"What? You need to watch your mouth!"

"No, fuck her! My daughter, *your* granddaughter wants something for Christmas and you're telling me to hold on so you can get someone something that isn't even your blood!" At the same time, he started arguing with my brother because he butted in, and they started going back and forth.

My dad raised up and started walking toward my brother and said, "You better watch your mouth! I'm your daddy regardless and you're going to respect me!"

I got up and grabbed my dad's shoulder and he threw his arm like he thought we were going to jump him, so I diffused the situation. We all sat down and talked. He apologized and we swept it under the rug. A couple days later they moved my dad. My dad came to the cell and told me he loved me and that they were moving him. When he moved, the G's kept asking me if I was going to join. I agreed to join partially for protection because my dad was gone, and partially for the idea that I could rise to the top and run it. I went through the initiation of reciting the pieces and the pledge and I was in. They threw a big party for me, and I was officially GD, a Gangsta Disciple.

I was only in for a few weeks and I already learned a lot. They quickly saw my potential and appointed me in a security position over my pod. I had a little authority. A brother got into some trouble within the gang, which is called a violation, while I was in my position, and they had to write him up. When someone was written up, it was my responsibility to turn in the report. The report required for him to do a six-minute no cover up. This meant that they sent three to four brothers in on a six-minute timer to beat him up, but he was allowed to fight back. I hadn't seen a violation before, and I thought the punishment was a little harsh. It was on me to decide what the punishment was going to be. BJ, my celly, told me it was my pod, so I had the authority to make whatever decision I wanted. I decided to change the time limit to three minutes instead of six minutes. When they saw he wasn't beat up that badly, the number one and number two over GD called me to ask me what happened. I told them that I was informed that it was my decision, and they wanted to know who gave me that information. They told me I was too fresh in the gang to be able to make those types of decisions. I told them it was my own decision.

They said, "Now listen lil bruh, don't lie to me. I can write you up for that and violate you for lying to a position of authority. Now when I ask you this last time, you need to tell me the truth. If you don't tell me the truth, I'll put you in violation and you'll be the one getting the six minutes."

When they asked me again, I told them the truth, that it was my celly BJ. BJ got in trouble and got a cover up, which is standing with your hands up for three minutes while they punched on him and he wasn't able to fight back. We fell out after that as cellies because he felt like I told on him. I switched

193

cells to the person who brought me in GD. BJ and I were at odds, and while all the brothers were gone to eat at chow, he went to the shower without telling me, and he went with his shower shoes on. Walking in your shower shoes was a security breach because they made you more vulnerable and you were required to wear your tennis shoes. So, when he walked back, I told him to come see me. He was a bigger guy and he had been GD for a long time so he thought he could just flex his muscles on me.

He walked in agressively and said, "What's up?"

I said, "How do you plead?"

"What do you mean?"

"You broke security. I saw you walk to and from the shower with your shower shoes on and no brothers are here, they're all at chow. You did not come and get me. How do you plead, guilty or not guilty?"

He asked me, "What? You're not doing no paperwork?"

I told him, "Ya'll taught me this. I can write it up or you can plead guilty right now and pay a fine to the box." The box was a place where we collected and ran a store for the brothers in the pod. The store operated on a two for one for outsider, meaning if they came to get anything, they had to pay back double when commissary ran. When the brothers went to the store, they only had to pay back what they owed, plus a two dollar a month due to help the box increase. I told him he could pay fifty dollars to the box or I could write it up and ask for a three-minute no cover up. He plead guilty and said he'd take the fifty-dollar fine and left. When the brothers got back from chow, I told my celly and he told me not to worry about it.

I still had my phone and the big to do was to get dope in through the visitation. I called home and asked a girl I was talking to for a long time if I could put her on someone else's visitation list and if she would bring some dope. She agreed. I asked another girl I was talking to if she would be her ride, and she agreed. I put her on a list for Little John who was known for sticking stuff in his butt. She brought me stuff three times; cocaine, weed, and cigarettes. I always gave the cigarettes to my celly to sell, and I sold the rest. We had about $400 in commissary. I was living in prison the same way I was accustomed to on the streets. I didn't learn the punishment that being locked up was supposed to teach you, I wasn't even thinking about my charge.

With my dad gone, I had to look after my brother, so I put in a request to have him moved to my cell. I felt like he went crazy and lost his mind. He had no filter and he was constantly saying something slick or reckless to somebody, and this was unlike him. He either wasn't mindful of how he spoke to people or he was so quiet that people thought something was wrong with him. It was one extreme or the other, no in-between. It seemed as if I had to be on watch for him all the time. One time my brother was playing really loud music during count time. Loud music wasn't allowed during this time or your cell could get searched. I had drugs and a cell phone in the cell, so I took the radio and put it under the bed. My brother went under the bed and took it back out, plugged it back up, and turned the music back on. When I tried to take it again, he tried to fight me, and I blacked out.

All the resentment I had built up from him not allowing me to wear his clothes, him spending his money on females or his friends, but never looking out for me, and never letting me drive his car, surfaced. He felt like he could just continue to run over me, and something came out of me that I didn't even know was there. We fought so bad I almost killed him. A rookie cop saw us fighting, but didn't know what to do, so he left us fighting in the cell while he called a higher badge. When they came to get us out of the cell, they threw both of us in the hole. My brother yelled out that I was tripping, but I was so angry and full of resentment that I told him he couldn't even come back to the compound.

After I got out, I kept getting drugs in for about three weeks. I got greedy and tried to get more than I normally got because I was making so much money, sending money home, living well, and had a lot of respect. Little John got caught because it was too big. When I found out, I moved all my stuff to a different place assuming he was going to tell on me, and they were going to come shake down my cell and put me in the hole. He didn't tell and he took the charge, but the girl went to jail and made bond. I never talked to her again. They wanted to discipline Little John because they felt like he messed up something that was benefiting all of us. I ruled against it because I thought by putting hands on him, it would land most of us in the hole. They removed me from my position because of my decision. They gave the position to BJ.

Later I was talking to another girl who I had known for some time. I didn't know that she moved on to talking to someone else, and that he wanted her to stop talking to me. The guy she was talking to called up to the prison and told them I had a cell phone. They came in while I was on the phone, caught me and wrote me up. I lost sixty of my good days because I got caught and written up. Good days are used towards behavior credits which can knock time off your sentence and get you out early. I was most upset because there weren't any cell phones on the compound, and if there were, they wanted $1000-

$1500 for it. By the time I got moved to a different cell, the price went down to $500 because someone had multiple phones.

Someone was letting me use their phone every now and then.

I let my neighboring cell mate use the phone one time and he said, "Man, we gotta get one of these."

I lied and told him the phone was going for $1000, and we could go half on it. The next day he had his five hundred and I bought the phone all while he thought we split the cost. I found another girl to bring me dope to the prison, and I found a GD who would smuggle it in. We had to keep it a secret because if the G's found out he was smuggling things in his butt then we'd both be in trouble. After he successfully brought some dope back, I decided I needed to be in a cell with him. Since his cell was upstairs, I put in a cell change request and moved in the cell with him. I was still sharing the phone with the guy who rightfully bought it until I decided I wasn't going to let him use it anymore.

I walked past him one day and he asked to use the phone. I said, "That's over with."

He looked at me and said, "What do you mean?"

"It's over with. I'm taking the phone."

He was what we called a "friend of GD." That meant he was close to someone who was Folk. It was a rule for all the brothers to work out twice a week, so while I was in the gym one day, one of the brothers pulled me to the side and brought up the phone situation.

He said, "Man you ain't straight for what you did."

"What are you talking about?"

"Bruh told me what happened, ya'll went half on a phone and you just quit letting him use the phone."

I told him, "That's none of your business. I don't know what he's talking about. If it is true, it's none of GD business, and it's none of your business, it's personal business." I walked off and kept working out. I saw the brother go back and talk to the guy I took the phone from and they both went to go talk to a guy that was higher authority. I watched knowing they weren't supposed to be doing that. They all pulled me to the side and I still denied it. I told them I was the one with the cell phone. The brother in position told me I wasn't right if I did do it because we didn't operate that way. I looked at him and said, "Look at me bruh, is this GD business?"

"No."

"It's personal business ain't it?"

"Yea, but it can come to the body and we can delegate."

I looked at the guy who rightfully bought the phone and asked him, "You wanna get em up?" That meant do you want to fight. I told him, "We can go in the cell and fight right now, if I win, I'm taking the phone, if not, it's a dead issue."

The guy said he didn't want to fight so I told them it was dead, walked off and went back to working out. A few days later they went and told the number one without following any proper procedure. He pulled me to the side and asked me about it, but I denied it again. I had brothers behind me telling him I didn't do it either, but only because they found out I had a phone and wanted to use it. I told the brothers to step out. I told the number one the truth about everything that happened thinking he was just going to throw it out. He wrote me up for lying and told me I had seventy-two hours to return the money, or return to the agreement that we had, or he was going to confiscate the phone himself. I told the brothers what happened, and they told me that he must've been paid because the guy's family had money.

Seventy-two hours was about to pass, and I came up with a plan that I would pay the guy his money back. The way we used money was on Green Dot cards which allowed money to be deposited to a set of numbers. The set of numbers could be added onto any card. I told my celly the plan was to load the card, call the G's in so they could verify the money was there and legitimate, and as soon as they walked out, use the numbers to put the money back on my card. My celly agreed to the plan. We called the G's in and they called the Green Dot card, put it on speaker and the automated system said there was $500 available on the numbers. I nodded to my celly after everybody walked out, and at the same time they called for rec. I went to rec with a bunch of the brothers and stayed outside. This was my alibi and I had witnesses to verify.

When we came back in from rec there were about eight G's standing at my door calling for me. I said, "What's up?"

"Man, you know what you did! You had us verify that money and then you pulled the numbers."

"Man, I been outside for the last hour." The brothers with me vouched for me.

The G's said, "I don't know how you did it, but you know what you did! You pulled those numbers."

"Well one of ya'll must've got the number because I didn't pull no numbers!" We started arguing. I was face to face with BJ. The guy that took me GD walked in and asked me what was going on. He tells all the brothers to step out so he could talk to me alone. I was angry crying because I felt like the GDs were taking someone else's side over mine. I was telling him the story with the lie that I didn't take the numbers and he stopped me.

"Man look at me lil homie." I looked at him. "I've been around you too long. I *know* you took those numbers."

I started laughing.

He said, "Man do something for me. Just give him the money. You're making money, just take the phone and give him the money."

I agreed and gave him the $500 and went back to getting money. Two days later BJ served me a violation for lying to a position of authority and a disorder of organization unity. That was one of the worst charges that I could get because it meant that I caused chaos between the brothers. He served me two different violations at two different times. The punishment for the lying to a position of authority resulted in me getting a three-minute no cover. I had to stand there with my hands up while they hit me for three minutes. The punishment for the disorder of organization unity could result in eradication, which meant they could check me in to the hole and beat me up or they could just take my membership and say I wasn't GD anymore.

My dad finally got a cell phone at the prison he was at, so I called him and told him what was going on. He told me that he was not allowed to serve me two different violations because that was double jeopardy. If he was going to serve me, it had to be all at one time because all of it happened on one occasion.

I started asking around to the brothers if BJ was allowed to serve me separately but because it wasn't something that anyone had seen before they all thought it was permissible. I reported back to my dad and he sent it up the chain of command at the prison he was at. When calls started coming in from higher ups at different prison, they called all the brothers in a cell and told us that there would be consequences for whoever took the issue to the heads outside of the prison because they didn't like when things weren't kept inhouse. I called my dad worried they would find out it was me and told him to call everything off. He told me I didn't have anything to worry about. I went in the cell with the one who took me GD, and he came up with the idea of me just taking the violation, then reporting that I was violated against the rules. He said I could get a higher up position, so I went in my cell and laid down to think about it.

The next morning, I went to BJ and told him I'd take a six-minute no cover to get it all over with. They gave me three days to prepare. I worked out, practiced and gassed myself up thinking I could whoop all of them. The day came and five people came to my cell: the timekeeper BJ, one brother on the bed for rotation in case someone got tired, and three brothers who were going to do the fighting. When BJ said "time," they all instantly rushed in. I kept my head covered and when I saw an opportunity to come up, I'd swing a few times and go back to keeping my head covered. After the third cycle, I came up to swing and someone hit me in my temple and knocked me over the toilet. It put me in a daze, and I tried to regain my consciousness, but I didn't keep my head covered. Another brother hit me in my head again and knocked me unconscious. I could see and hear but I was completely out. They picked me up off the ground by my arms and kept punching me and hitting me in my body, chest and face.

I heard one of the brothers say, "Man he's knocked out, I'm not finna keep hitting him."

BJ kept telling them to go. Another brother said I needed a TP which meant they could take a break so I could get myself together. With the little strength I had I told them I didn't want a TP and to get it over with. They kept going until the six-minute mark. I was bleeding, busted up, and swollen. They shook my hand as they left. One of the brothers came to check on me and asked me if was I okay.

I told him, "Call my momma and tell her I'm ready."

He said, "What?"

"Call my momma and tell her she can come get me, I'm ready."

He whistled for one of the brothers and told him they might have to take me to the clinic. I started laughing and told them I was just playing, and I was okay, I just wanted some food. While I was eating, I told my celly I was going to kill all of them. I got an order from the higher up not to sell any of them cocaine because none of us needed to be using, but I told my celly, "Every single one of them niggas that want some cocaine, I'm selling it to them and lacing it with battery acid." I never served any of them because I ended up on probation for a year which meant I couldn't be in any incidents or get any write ups or I would be removed from the body immediately. The brothers who didn't like me used it as an opportunity to mess with me and get me out of character because I had to walk a fine line. It was killing me.

They called me in a cell one day, and when I walked in, some of the brothers getting high. I couldn't say anything because I knew they wanted to use it to flip around on me and get me removed from GD. A few days later I was in a cell with the higher ups and the third top GD came in and asked me step out. As I was leaving, I heard him say he took it upon himself to sanction himself for failing the drug test. I stepped back in the cell and asked him to repeat himself. He told me to leave so he could speak to them privately. I said, "No, because it sounded like I heard you say you were using. That's supposed to be a write up, and we're all supposed to know about that. I haven't seen a write up."

He said, "Man just leave, we'll handle it and get everything together."

"No, how about I call a meeting when the brothers get back from chow so we can all discuss it because we all need to know about this, and I want to see the write up." To be written up for using meant an automatic removal from your position and six-minute cover up. Before the brothers came back, he called me in the cell and asked me what I wanted to do. I told him, "It's not about what I want to do, it's about what the memo says for you to do. You're supposed to be removed from your position and get a six-minute cover up. How are you going to lead me when you're a junky around here getting high off cocaine?" He told me I was being disrespectful for calling him a junky.

We called the brothers in the cell and the brothers who used cocaine believed I had a personal agenda because I didn't get high. They thought I was trying to get a spot, and I was mad because I was on probation. I got mad and went off, and they wrote me up for disrespect. They called me to the side to discuss the write up and the three heads said they'd dismiss the write up if I left the situation alone. I got bamboozled again so they could do what they wanted to do. They started an investigation on me for sending one of the brothers up to bring dope in. They did this because I wouldn't serve them, so I quit getting dope in.

I started working out a lot. I was on the yard one day and Tony was out there too. We were playing basketball and I was talking trash to a Crip that we were playing against. It got so heated that another

Crip joined in and started talking crazy to me too. I took it personal, "Man, I don't know who the fuck you think you talking to, you ain't going to do shit to me." It immediately turned into a hostile environment for the G's and the Crips. All of them were standing at attention.

One of the Crips said, "When we get in there, we can fall in the cell!"

I replied, "Fall in the cell? What are we going to fall in the cell for when we have all this space and opportunity? We can fall in right now." After I said this, I knew I had to win. We went off to the side of the building for my first fight. I was winning the fight, and my last punch, I hit him I his eye and split it. When he started bleeding one of the G's broke it up. Some of the Crips came to the door of the cell and said he wanted to fight again.

About six G's went to the door and told them, "Ain't gon be no more fighting, he might as well cough that up as a loss. If anybody think they going to come over here and do anything to lil Joe T, they better bring their knives. It's over with."

They left it alone. I knew right then the G's did not play.

I decided to make one more dope run even though I stopped selling it, but I didn't have a ride for the girl to bring it. I went to the OG Crip who was over all the Crips because I knew he went to visitation all the time. I told him I'd cut him in if he had his girlfriend bring the girl who had the dope. He agreed because he wanted to get some morphine pills in. I was using his phone because mine was broken, and when I used his phone, I saw he was texting the girl who was bringing me dope, trying to talk to her. I took the phone to my cell for privacy, and I called the girl. When she answered I said, "I have one question. Did he try to holla at you or are you trying to holla at him?" She immediately broke down crying, told me what happened and apologized. I went back to his cell and closed the door because I had the intent on beating him up for disrespecting me. I didn't care what gang or what position he was in. I asked him, "I got one question for you. Did you call her, or did she call you?"

"What you talking about Lil Joe?"

As he was saying this, he grabbed his shower shoes and his towel and walked out. I immediately went to the G's to tell them what was going on, how he disrespected me, and how I was going to take his phone and not give it back. Since I lost credibility, they thought I set it all up just so I could take his phone. When he got out the shower, I sent the G's to tell him the only way he was getting his phone back was if we fought, and they came back and told me he didn't want to fight. Not only was he an OG Crip but he was kin to one of the people who had the top three positions in GD. I knew this was going to be a problem.

They came to my cell to tell me they were going to confiscate the phone to give it back to him. Tony just became Crip and when he caught wind of it, he came to talk to me. I told him what happened. He asked me what I wanted to do because I gave him stuff sometimes too. I told him I wanted to whoop him. He went to go get some of the big homies of

Crip and brought them to the cell, they called the G's to the cell, and they began discussing the situation.

Tony interrupted and said, "Man fuck all that. What you wanna do Joe T?"

I said, "I'm finna beat the shit outta him."

They asked the OG Crip what he wanted to do and if he wanted to fight. He said he didn't. When he said that, the Crips told us to leave, and before we were even out of the door, they beat him up. We could hear him in the cell screaming. When I went to my cell, Tony came over with blood on his shirt to tell me it was over with. He got removed from Crip. Tony took his phone, so the guy had to go downstairs to use the collect phone. Tony went in his cell to beat him up again for a reason unknown. When he came to my cell again with blood on his shirt, he took his shirt off, left it in my cell, and went back to his unit. The guy got beat up badly and went downstairs to use the phone.

I had a feeling he was telling, and shortly after the police came locking down, and searching cells.

When they came to search my cell, they caught me trying to throw Tony's bloody shirt away. The shirt had his inmate numbers on it, indicating it belonged to him, so they locked both of us up in the hole. Tony took the charge, so they were going to let me out of the hole. Before they let me out a war erupted between the Crips and the G's with both gangs stabbing each other. That resulted in the entire compound being locked down. Since it was lock down, I couldn't get out the hole until the lockdown was lifted. As I was waiting in the hole, they shipped half of the Crips and half of the G's to different prisons. By the time I got out of the hole, there were a lot of new G's and they were trying to restructure the administration. They asked me if I wanted to get in the vote to have one of the top three spots. I declined because at that point I felt betrayed by the G's. One of the G's I was close to that I knew had a good heart ended up getting the top position. He pulled me to the side to inform me that they made a call on me to remove me from the body and check me in the hole by means of protective custody. They didn't like me, and they felt as if I put Tony up to it and created a war between gangs. He told me it was a dead issue since there was new administration and it was his call.

Another year passed and I was going on five years and my dad was trying to get me in with him at the prison he was at. While I was waiting to switch prisons, I moved to a different area and was given a position, but I was tired of being there and I wanted to get out. I talked with another G, Looney, who also wanted to get out. One of the top positions came to me and asked what we were talking about and Looney mentioned he wanted to "get off count," but the top position told him he needed to "plug out." Plugging out was removing yourself from GD. Getting off count was removing yourself from the structure of how the operated. The position told him it was the same thing, so Looney went and wrote up his paperwork that he wanted to plug out. He grabbed a knife from the Crips because he was scared, so the Folks said that he bared arms against the Folk.

They made a call on him and sent three people to beat him up, but he beat all three of them up. He started talking crazy, so when he went back to his cell, they sent two more people to jump him. They took his knife and stabbed him three times. He got checked in to the hole because they stabbed him. He signed some papers to come back out to the unit, so the brothers talked to me about it since it was my call on what I wanted to do. I called an open discussion and got all the brothers outside.

Before we met, I called and asked the number three who I was close to if he made the call because he was the only on in a position to do so. He told me somebody else made the call and when he found out it was already done, he was asked to back the guy up who made the call if anybody asked. He thought me made the right decision, and I told him that he didn't. I told him I was going to go to the open discussion and vouch for Looney to stay in the unit. He told me he'd back me up, so I went to open discussion and explained how Looney was misinformed by one of the brothers, was manipulated, and lied to. They guy who lied and manipulated Looney started telling his side, but he was lying. He fixed his story up so well that it infuriated me. I stepped to him, put my fingers

217

in his face and told him, "You a bitch ass nigga." I looked at everyone else and told them, "Ya'll gon keep letting this mutha fucker be the leader over us and he's lying." I balled my fist up like I wanted to hit him so one of the brothers grabbed me and walked me off. He wrote me up for disrespect. I refused to take the violation and a lot of brothers were standing with me because they knew he was wrong.

I was so tired of the way things were operating and the way administration was running. I wrote up my plug out papers and kept it in my pocket until another incident occurred. They came to my cell to tell me what happened, but I reached in my pocket and handed them my plug out papers. They asked me if I was sure, but I was willing to take whatever came with it because I was tired. I told them to run it up the chain of command. When they left, I started praying, and I called my dad. My dad told me he wished I would've waited until I got there with him. A few days later they came to my cell to tell me I was out, and it was finished. I went outside to the yard and motioned to the number one that I was finished. He motioned back that I was good to go. So, to make

218

a statement to the unit that I was done, I took my shower shoes and walked to the shower.

A few weeks later I got moved to the jail my dad was at. When I got there, they moved me to opposite end of the compound of where my dad was. After a week they moved me to the same cell as my dad; we were cell mates. After he helped me move all my stuff in, we sat and watched TV and talked. I told him about what happened at the prison I came from, and he told me what operation he had going on at this prison. He told me I could sign up for the wood plant which was about $300-$400 a week, so I signed up and got the job. I learned how to play chess, so I played chess with my dad in the cell. I told him my old stories and he told me how crazy he thought I was. He told me some of his old stories, about my mom, how they met, when I was born, all kinds of stories.

He had two cell phones and he kept telling me he would give me one, but he never did. He kept the second phone put up just in case the main phone was found and confiscated. He talked to his girlfriend all the time. When he got off work, all he wanted to do was talk to her, and it seemed as if I couldn't get him to do anything. We got in an argument because he wouldn't let me use the phone. When he went to work, I went to the cell where I knew he was keeping the phone and asked the guy to let me use the phone. The guy told me he didn't keep the phone there anymore, so I asked him again. He told me he didn't have anything to do with what my dad and I had going on, so I grabbed him and choked him. He got away so I went back to my cell. When my dad got off work, he told him what happened. My dad tried to tell me I couldn't do that, but I wasn't hearing him. I didn't like him having me on a restriction after bringing me all that way and not allowing me to use the phone. While we were arguing he asked me to step out and give him privacy. He turned his back to me, and I could tell he was going to cry. When he turned his back, I grabbed his shoulder and asked him, "What's up?"

He threw his arm trying to get me off him. "I know you don't love me. I know I've been gone all your life. I know you don't have any respect for me..."

He kept going on and on. I told him, "Look, I love you, but I don't think you understand. My momma had to raise us. My uncles didn't do much. They brought us to come see you, but they never did much for us. Now I'm sitting in a cell with you and you don't really understand how much resentment I have towards you. I joined Folk because of you, I got in the dope game because of you, and even hearing stuff about you as I was growing up, I wanted to be that."

We went back and forth until everything calmed down and we finally sat down. He hugged me and told me he was sorry and that he meant it. He said he never had anyone who was right there with him as he pointed at his eyes. He told me they didn't understand him. He had been gone for a long time, and he couldn't call home to talk to people he used to grow up with. He only had a little bit of family left. He said nobody had been right there with him that understood. I had been in prison for about three or four years, so I told him I understood. We squashed everything right there and formed the best father son relationship we could have under the circumstances.

A few days later while on the way to work, one of the inmates came to get me to tell me we had a new guard. She was an Indian woman, and in my mind, I was going to get her. A few days later she came to work our unit and introduced herself to everyone. I went a few days ignoring her and playing it cool because I knew every guy there was going to be trying to get her attention. While I was walking to get ice one day, she tried to stop me to talk. She was in the cage and I told her I didn't come to the cage. I told her if she had anything to say she could ask me from there. She asked me who was in the cell with me, and I told her it was my dad.

She said, "I thought so because I could see both of your names on there and his is junior and yours is the third."

I told her, "You're just trying to start conversation." She started laughing. She later came upstairs to stand in front of me and my dad's door. I still played hard to get even though I knew she liked me. I was walking past one day, and she stopped me again. I told her she knew I wasn't coming to the cage.

She pointed at somebody and I told her, "Don't point at people when you're talking to me, that makes me look like the police."

She asked me, "Who's that dude right there?"

I told her I didn't know.

She said, "I'm kinda scared of him. He looks like he'll do something to me. He looks like one of those guys who will throw me in the cell and rape me."

I was shocked and said, "You think he'd do that for real?"

She said yes. I told her not to worry about him and when she came in the next morning, he'd be moved. She admonished me not to get in any trouble. but I told her I had it under control. I went to the cell and told my dad what she said. He had some Suboxone strips which were being sold for $150 a piece. I had someone go talk to the guy the officer referenced and tell him he'd get one of the pills if he checked himself in to the hole. He agreed so he told the police he feared for his life. They packed him up and sent him to the hole. When the officer saw he was gone and checked her roster, she flew upstairs and knocked on my door. She opened the door and stood outside the cell. Women officers weren't allowed in the cell unless they had backup.

She asked me, "What did you do?"

I said, "What are you talking about?"

"He's not in here anymore, where is he?"

"Oh, he checked himself into the hole."

"How did you do that?"

"The only thing you need to worry about is that I said he wasn't going to be here anymore." She looked, and told me thank you, and walked off. I would flirt with her after that. One day I was playing chess and I was trash talking. When I won, the guy walked off mad, and I backed up to the officer and started talking to her. I said, "Don't respond to what I'm going to say. What if we could talk outside of here?" She didn't say anything. I said, "I think you know what I mean. I'm going to go in the staff bathroom and put my number under the sink. When you get ready to leave tonight, go get the number, and you can call me blocked. But if I go in the staff bathroom in the morning and the number is still there, we'll act like we never had this conversation." I walked off.

I went upstairs and put the number under the sink. I told my dad I was keeping the phone in the cell that night. He told me I was going to take all the charges if I got caught, and I was okay with that. That night she came and did her count, and when she came to my cell, she threw her thumb up. My dad asked me what that meant, and I played dumb. When she came back by to check to see if the doors were locked, she stuck her head in and told me she got it.

My dad looked at me and said, "What the hell you got going on?"

I told him the truth and he told me I might as well get ready to go to the hole because the police were coming in the next thirty minutes. I disagreed, but he didn't care so long as I was taking all the charges. We watched her leave work, and an hour and a half later I got a phone call from a restricted number. She told me she was just calling to see if the number worked and that she still wanted to talk to me later. We hung up the phone.

After that she would offer me some of her food, and eventually I told her what kind of food I wanted, and she would bring it. We talked on the phone every night. We got to a point where I was telling her how much money I could make off narcotics, cocaine, weed, pills, tobacco or whatever. She told me she would bring everything except pills in with her and asked me what I wanted. I told to bring me weed and she brought me ounces of weed at a time. We got so close I bought a ring and proposed to her. At some point somebody started telling on us, because they thought that I was getting people moved in and out of the unit so the officer and I could be in charge.

The Vice Lords said they felt like I had all their cells searched. I did, but nobody knew about it. When they came in from the yard one day, they were at a standoff with the Crips and I filled the officer in on what was happening. There were some Vice Lords who were getting weed in too, so I thought to use it as an opportunity to get them moved out of the unit altogether. I told her which cells I thought needed to be searched just so I could get the monetary advantage. She made a call to the green team who conducts the cell searches and they searched eight Vice Lord's cells; six of them went to the hole. One of the Vice Lords thought it was me and spread a rumor that I was responsible and needed to be checked in. The rumor made it to my dad. My dad came to wake me up and told me to put my shoes on. I followed him to a cell where all the Vice Lords were, and we had the G's with us.

My dad said to the guy who started the rumor, "Tell my son everything you've been telling us."

"I'm not trying to say he's a rat, snitch, or the police or anything, I'm just saying I think he was being a little too friendly with that officer and ended up saying something that got my brothers' cell searched."

I said, "So, you are trying to say I'm the police, right?"

He said, "No, I'm just saying you may be a little too close to the girl and feel like you can tell her certain things that got us searched."

I told him he was going to get it, so they patted us both down, we fought, I beat him up, choked him out, and busted his head. One of the Vice Lords told me one of the Crips was saying the same thing, so I walked down to his cell to check him, but he said he didn't have anything to do with it. The next day they sent someone to our cell to buy Suboxone. I asked him who told him, and he pointed out the cell and told me who told him. It was one of the Crips. I went to the OG who was over them and told him one of his people was telling random dudes that my dad had drugs for sale. He didn't think he did it, so we got the dude, he got some Crips, and we took some G's to the guys cell.

I told the guy who came to buy the drugs, "Now tell them what you told me. Who told you we had those drugs?" He pointed him out.

The Crip said, "Man I ain't told you nothing like that. You're lying!"

He reached and tried to smack him, and I grabbed him.

"You ain't finna make me feel like he didn't tell me the truth, just because he's not affiliated." He kept trying to plead his case, so I said, "Fuck all that." I turned around and smacked the guy who came to our cell asking for drugs. He fell and I picked him back up and smacked him again and pushed him out the cell. I told him, "Don't you ever come to my door asking for drugs again." I turned around and told the Crip, "Now, I'm finna whoop your ass." When I reached to grab him, one of the Crips grabbed my hand to stop me. I told him, "Your homeboy telling people we have drugs and he could've got my cell searched. I'm finna beat his ass."

He said, "No, we're not doing that, we deal with our own."

We left the cell and they beat him up. After that it seemed to be incident after incident. My dad and I laughed about it because he said I carried myself just like he did. I was still working at the plant, and my girl, the officer was still bringing in dope. I saved up around $6000-$7000. I felt like a real king.

Then the green team started messing with me and my dad. The officer brought me two ounces and I told her it was going to be the last time. She came to my cell and told me the weed was in the spot, so I sent my homeboy downstairs to go get it. She walked by the door and winked at me. I was curious what that meant. The guy came back with the weed and I told him to go to several different cells with the weed before putting it in the correct cell, which was Tiny's cell. This was so if they searched anything, they'd have to search them all. When he came back, he sat down in the cell with me. Not even fifteen minutes passed before one of the officers went to the last cell he went to, my cell, and my friend's cell. The last cell they went to was Tiny's cell. My dad got off work while they were searching and asked what was going on. I told him everything was in the cell they were searching. There were 200 pills, two ounces of weed, and two cell phones.

I asked my dad, "If a fight breaks out right now, what are they going to do?" He told me they'd have to come out and stop the fight. I sent my friend down to tell the guy I'd give him five Suboxone if he started a fight right then. The guy looked at me, and I gave him a nod of approval. He immediately punched the first person he saw and started a fight. They came out and locked the door and stopped the fight. They cuffed them and took them out of the unit. As they were on their way out, my girl asked if they were done searching, and in the heat of the moment, they said they were finished. She ran up and unlocked the cell. We got everything out and moved it around, so we got away with it.

A few days later they put my dad on pending investigation. When he got out the hole, they told him to pack his bag because he was going back to pending investigation. He packed his stuff up and went back to the hole. A week later they told me they were moving him to another prison, but nobody knew why. The truth was they felt like with my dad out of the picture, I'd slip up with the officer and get caught. It broke my heart when they moved him. I ended up moving one of my friends from Springfield in the cell with me. The first couple of days were rough on me, but I realized I had to keep it moving whether he was there or not.

On my way to work one day, green team searched my cell. They said they had an anonymous tip that I had a cell phone in my cell. While I was at work, they called me back to my cell to search it again. I felt like I was being harassed so I went to talk to someone about it. They told me they were getting tips and when they receive tips, they must search the cell. As I'm sitting in my cell, someone got jumped and stabbed so I knew we were going on lockdown. I put my cell phone up but kept four or five thimbles of weed in my pocket. When they came in, I didn't think they were going to search any cells because someone just got stabbed. They came in the pod and came straight to my cell.

They came in and said, "How are you doing, Mr. Baker."

I jumped down off the bunk, "I'm good, what's going on?"

"Put your hands up, let me pat you down."

"For what? There's a guy down there who just got stabbed and you're going to search my cell?"

"Yea, we're going to search it."

I reached to grab the weed out of my pocket so I could flush it, but he grabbed my hand before I could. He said, "If you move again it'll be assault on an officer."

"Man, just let me flush it, it's only some cigarettes."

"well if it's cigarettes, give it to me and I'll flush it."

He finally got me to open my hand and I got written up for contraband. I was going back and forth to the DBoard where they delegate your punishment for write ups, and the green team wanted to talk to me. All they wanted to talk about was the woman officer, but I denied any allegations. As we were going back and forth, they brought me food, but I still told them I didn't know anything, and I denied knowledge of what they were talking about. They told me the warden gave them permission to drop the write up if I gave up the officer. They told me I was going to lose my job and my good time for the month. They brought up my daughter and the fact I had parole coming up and it wasn't going to look good, but I didn't care about any of it. My celly was going to try to take the charge, but they wouldn't allow it.

Two months passed and I wanted to plead guilty to the possession of contraband. The green team told me the warden gave orders not to allow me to plead guilty. They tried to bribe me with anything I wanted. They asked me if I wanted my dad moved back or if I wanted to move to the prison he was at. They told me they could have us back as cell mates as early as the next day. I asked them, "Is it that serious?"

"Look, I don't have a problem with you or what you do to survive in here. I have a problem with an officer that comes in and puts my other officer's lives in jeopardy. She could have given you any information on any of the officers outside of here and that's a threat to my security. I'm going to have her removed and red flagged, so she'll never be able to work for the state again."

I still denied that I knew anything. They continued to harass me. I spoke with the counselor and the counselor spoke to the assistant warden. When I got called to the warden's office to talk, Internal Affairs was present. They offered the same bribery the green team offered me. I told them to call the warden, and I'd take the deal.

The warden came in and asked, "Is there anything you want to tell me?"

I said, "Yea, your Internal Affairs are harassing me, your green team is harassing me, and you have people all over the compound thinking I'm the police. They're threatening my job, and I've had a write up pending for two months. They won't allow me to plead guilty based off a command from your assistant warden. I wanted to ask you personally, what is going on with your administration?"

She said she was unaware of everything that was going on and asked me what I wanted to do. I told her I wanted to be shipped to a different prison.

Internal Affairs stood up and said, "He's full of shit! He told us he wanted you down here because he had information about the officer that's under investigation."

The warden asked me if I had anything going on with an officer that worked there and when I told her no, she told me I could leave. Later that day they called me to the clinic. When I got to the clinic, green team called me to the back where inmates weren't allowed. They pulled out a cell phone and told me the warden told them they weren't allowed to give it to me, but they would ship me out tonight if I called and got confirmation from the officer that we had been communicating. I told them once again I didn't have anything to do with the allegations they were making. I told them that it wasn't the warden that wanted me to do what they were asking, but they were at their last straw because I was being shipped off. He asked me once more if I would do it and I refused.

I went back to my cell and called all the gangs in the cell. I told them, "This might sound crazy and I've never told anyone, but that officer is my girl. That ring on her finger, I gave it to her. They're talking about searching my cell tonight, making it look like they found a cell phone, taking me down to the hole, then making me call her to get her caught up. I don't know what else they plan on doing or who else cells they plan on searching, but ya'll need to tell ya'll people if they have anything, it needs to be put up and secure."

I went back to my cell and when my friend came up from working in the kitchen, I started reminiscing about everything and talked about everything I was going to miss about the place. I got really close to the officer. We would kiss and when I would fake to go take the trash out, we would freak and go on about our day. As I was talking someone said, green team is on the block. They came and searched two cells where I used to keep everything. They acted like they found a cell phone and they pointed to my cell. They came in and made my celly squat and cough. They told me I didn't really have to squat and cough, I just needed to make it sound like I did. They were going to take my stuff and set it in the cage so it would appear I got checked in, and I could use the phone and make the call.

They took me to operations, gave me the phone and told me to call her. I told them I didn't know the number. They pulled out a list of numbers and I pointed to another number I knew to an officer that was bringing in dope to another inmate. They asked me how I knew the number and I gave the inmate's name to get the heat off me and told them that officer was bringing in dope to that inmate.

One officer said, "I knew it!"

I told them that's how I got all the dope. Some of the officers still didn't believe me. I wanted to see if the phone worked so I text my sister, and she texted back. I text my mom and she texted back telling me it was late, and I needed to put my phone up. I texted my celly's girlfriend who I let hold some of my money and asked if she told my girl because beforehand, I told her to tell her what was going on. I deleted all the texts. They saw me text and delete the messages. I said, "It'll seem really strange that it's two in the morning, and I haven't been checked into the hole, and I have proof by texting everybody that ya'll let me use the phone, which shows foul play was going on. Yea, I'm calling my lawyer first thing in the morning."

The head of green team said, "You wouldn't!"

I said, "Try me!"

"Lock his ass up!"

They threw me in the hole and didn't give me any of my property. They let the inmates steal all my stuff, from commissary to hygiene stuff. I flooded the cell and when they opened the door, I told them to bring me my TV. They brought my TV and a few of my belongings. I stayed in the hole thirty days, I couldn't get a haircut and my facial hair grew out. They put me on a bus and moved me back to the prison where it all started, where my uncle was. When I got there that prison was on lockdown because an officer got jumped on and stabbed. I asked an officer if they knew my uncle and they said he was in the unit

I was going to. I felt the biggest relief I had felt my entire time in prison because I was tired and ready to give in. I was tired of hustling, tired of gang banging, tired of trouble, and I knew my uncle changed his life. I thought to myself, "God if this is you, take the wheel… cause I'm tired."

Chapter 8: Change

When I got there that's when things began to change. I was walking through the unit contemplating which direction I really wanted to go. I didn't know if I wanted to get with my uncle and try to better my life since I had about three years left, or if I wanted to get around some dudes who were living the same way I was living before I got there; getting my hands on cell phones, drugs, and whatever I needed to make my time easy. As I was walking to the unit, some guy asked me if I was Joe Baker, I was wondering how he knew who I was. He said he would be back to talk to me. I didn't know if it was good or bad, but I was going to defend myself either way.

I asked which cell my uncle was in, and they pointed to the one in the corner. I went to his cell and knocked on his door. He came to the door and I asked him, "You know who I am?"

He said, "Naw… you look familiar."

"Man, you don't know who I am?"

"Tommy?"

That was my dad's nickname, and he thought I was my dad. I told him I was his nephew, Boo. He asked me if I was still affiliated and I told him that passed a while ago. He asked me if I knew he changed his life, and I told him I heard about it.

He said, "If you're done being affiliated and you want to get your life on the right track, I'll do anything I can to help you… but if you're still on that mess I can't do nothing for you. It's different over here, these are some different types of dudes. Dudes are conniving and cutthroat here. So, if you're going to be with it, you need to be all the way with it. If you want out and you want to chill, I got you. I'll do anything I can to help you."

I told him right there I was through. He told me as soon as they opened the doors, we were going to go down and get me whatever job I wanted and figure it out from there. I was in the cell with someone I was in the group home with for a month before my uncle's best friend moved me in a cell with him. My uncle came to our cell one day and asked me if I could rap. I told him I could and let him hear something.

Before the song finished, he said, "Naw nephew, we aint rapping about that stuff no more."

You need to rap about something positive in a positive way. They had a rap group called RAW which stood for Radical Anointed Worship. He told me if I came up with something positive, he'd let me perform it at the church. I spent days thinking about it, and I already missed my old life. Trying to do the right thing for that small amount of time seemed boring and made time move slow. I started trying to do stuff behind my uncle's back with some of the money I had left over. I tried to get a cell phone and it didn't work, it got caught up. I tried to get some weed and it didn't work, it got caught up. Anything I was trying to get my hands on wasn't working.

I started going down to the church with my uncle every time they had service. Most of the guys had life sentences. As I watched them, I noticed it was something different about them and they had a peace about themselves. I know we're all flawed, and we all fall short, but they were different. It was different to me because I was accustomed to being around guys that tried to get one over on you. They weren't trying to get one over on me and they were serious about me trying to better my life.

My uncle came to my cell and told me he wanted to pray for me. I thought he was just going to pray but he reached for my hands and said to touch and agree. I didn't know much about the bible, but I agreed. When he started praying it made me emotional because it was the first time that I heard someone pray over my life and it took me back to the moment when I knew the Lord came into my heart. I was on maximum security and I was stressing a lot. I was going through the channels on the TV and came to the TBN station. When I saw it was a black preacher, I stopped. It was TD Jakes. His preaching touched on how wrong I was living and that I needed a Savior. I started watching him every day at 5:00, and on Sundays. I got off my bed and started pacing the floor, talking to God the way I knew how, and I got on my knees. I got on my knees and I started praying. As I was praying, I started speaking in a different language. When I got up and looked in the mirror and asked myself, "What was that?"

Every night after that I would pray and start speaking in a different language. Looking back at that moment I knew I received what they say is the Holy Spirit. I felt like even though I didn't know Him or the Word, He protected me my entire ride through prison because I went without being seriously hurt, stabbed or jumped on. It was grace and mercy that allowed me to get through prison the way I got through. It was a breeze in comparison to other guys. When my uncle walked out the cell, I told myself, "I've tried everything else, I'm going to give God a try." I decided to get serious.

When I performed my first song, I got a lot of positive feedback, so I decided to keep making music. Every time I performed the church would be packed. As people left, a lot of people told me they came to hear me rap, so I kept going. I had a parole date coming up and because I was building my relationship with God, I thought He was going to open doors and let me go home. When I went to my parole hearing, I wasn't in there five minutes before it got denied. They told me I had to serve the remaining balance which was another two years. The walk back to my unit was the longest walk. I remember thinking to myself, "Instead of getting my hopes up for nothing and thinking God is going to do something for me because I'm going to church, and trying to do right, I'd rather go back to what I was doing." My uncle and my friend came to check on me, but I wouldn't come out my cell for three days.

My celly asked me what I was going to do, and I told him I was going to write a book. He started laughing, but I told him to pass me my pen and paper. I stayed up day and night writing and wrote the first fourteen chapters of my book within the first seven days. I was writing a fiction book with different characters. Because I didn't know the bible that well, I'd ask my celly for the best fitting scripture based on the conversation the characters were having. After he gave me a couple scriptures, I started studying them. My uncle taught me how to use the concordance and as I started looking up the words in the original language, I began to really understand the Word. I got so intrigued with the Bible I wanted to read it every day. I wanted to know as much as possible, get to know God, and really find myself, who I was becoming and what I was going to be. I studied the bible like an addiction.

As I talked about my books, I would talk about the ministry God was going to birth called Life Ministries because God was showing me stories that I could relate to my old life. I always called my old life *the* life. I kept going to church and building my relationship with God. By the time I was at this prison for two years, I started going to a barber school to learn how to cut hair. I got close to a lot of these brothers and they were a part of the body of Christ as well. We'd throw parties and have luncheons. I had an experience with Cairos which was amazing. Cairos was a spiritual event that lasted three days where men could fellowship and testify and play games, eat, pray, etc. The way they treated us, the food, and everything we learned made it a great must have experience.

Fights started breaking out on the compound a lot. We were on constant lock down for days and sometimes even weeks. We were on lock down for two months once. It got so bad that they started moving loads of people to different prisons. We initially thought it was because of the fights but we soon found out it was because they were shutting down part of the prison and turning it into a women's prison. The first forty brothers they moved were all a part of the church. My uncle and my celly were some of the first people on the list. My uncle came to my cell and told me he was leaving in the morning. It devasted me in the same way it did when my dad got moved. I laid in my cell talking to God, "I don't understand what's going on. Every time I get close to somebody or I get comfortable things get shaken up." Even in going to prison it seemed like I couldn't get comfortable because I got moved to seven different prisons in my ten-year prison sentence which was unheard of. I questioned God, "Why am I always being put in an uncomfortable situation?"

When they moved my uncle, they moved me to a different unit, and my celly was another brother from the body of Christ. After a few months our names got put on the list to move to a different prison. I was willing to go to any prison in the state except the prison I just came from. I didn't want to go there because I felt like I made a lot of progress, made a lot of change, and avoided a lot of circles I didn't want to be in. I knew by going back, there wouldn't be the same level of accountability or the people who were trying to live right. I knew the type of environment I would have to go into. Two days later the counselor told me I was moving back to the prison. I started praying hard.

The day came for us to get moved. We got there and when they put us on the compound, I saw people I knew from other prisons that immediately approached me. They wanted to know what I was trying to do assuming I was going to get back in the game. I told them I was finished, and I gave my life to Christ. I was *finished*. They didn't believe me, so I told them that I had a written a couple of books, and that I got out of the affiliation. I explained my experience at the prison I was transferring from, and I didn't want any part of my old lifestyle. They respected it. I believe they respected it because of the way that I carried myself and lived a changed life the duration of my sentence. My name wasn't out there, I didn't beat anybody up, I didn't owe any debts. Word spread around the compound that I was a believer and I wasn't living the same lifestyle anymore, so everyone respected the fact and left it alone.

After being there a few months, I got my first book published by sending it back home and having someone send it to the publisher. I gave it out to a few of the prisoners, officers, and the counselor. That gave my name further respect. A lot of people came to me for prayer or when they needed something. God was still blessing me and providing for me, so I had a lot of material things. I had a lot of hygiene products and commissary. People on the outside were helping me a lot more than when I was in my alternative lifestyle. Now that I was living right, God blessed me with people that would be there for me when I needed something. I was also seeing a girl that came to see me every week. She did a lot of things for me that other people weren't willing to do like sending money, coming to see me, making phone calls, helping me with my books, writing me, sending me pictures, everything.

I went back up for parole when I still had a year left. They denied me again and told me to finish the remaining time. It didn't take a toll on me the same way it did the first time. I ended up buying myself a cell phone, but I didn't have any incidents like I used to have. It seemed as if God was testing me to see if I was going to stand without the previous prison's structure and accountability, and I actually stood on the Word more. It pushed me to read more and study more. It forced me to hold on to it more because it was something I didn't want to lose.

I went through a couple cell mates but by the grace of God I didn't get any bad ones. Things happened at the prison that put us on lockdown, but it didn't affect me. I was so close to getting out and I was so focused on my books, ministry, and letting people see that change was possible. I knew I wasn't the same person I used to be, and I didn't want to treat people the same way I used to treat them. I didn't view people the same way, I now saw them as souls. I could tell God changed my heart. The way I talked and walked and conducted myself. I knew it wasn't the prison experience or being afraid because I lived that life. I knew it was the fact that I was tired, and I found a new way of living. It's easy to be evil, as easy as turning on a switch. It's easy to be that way and find people who will accept you being that way, and even find people to be *with* you while you're that way because it's so easy.

It's harder to be different, but I realized it was worth it. It was worth the struggle, trials, and tribulations. It was worth being able to look in the mirror and see a different person.

Around thirty days left I took the phone I had and started recording some of the interaction of the prison. I wanted to take it home with me and share it with the youth so they could see that the way prison is presented and puffed up, is not a reality. I remember calling home and the way I talked about prison made it seem like I had it easy. I didn't realize that I wasn't calling home warning people that the truth was, this was a place no one wanted to come to. If you were sent to hell, how would you call home and describe it? Would you call home and say it was fun because there were certain aspects about it that you liked?

I felt like I was in a place that was literally hell. I had to see people get stabbed, kill themselves, overdose on drugs, people becoming addicts who never did drugs before, women getting beat up, and guards getting jumped on. I had to see people get fired from their jobs for bringing drugs in, or having sex with inmates, con artist, manipulators, homosexuality, all kinds of things. It was a place of complete chaos. It was a modern-day Sodom and Gomorrah. There were no aspects of prison that were good or okay. The way they treat you, your food portioning, the way you're treated at the visitation gallery, the way you had to strip down, the way your family had to strip down, was all a bad experience. The education was poor and there's no way to get the education you needed where you could come home and be able to be successful. No computers or a way to obtain computer skills, no life skills, or anything. Prison should never be described in a way that is good.

I was in there ten years and I didn't even realize how fast time is going or how far I'd be behind. I remember telling my dad it was like time stopped. You get stuck in the year that you got arrested and went to prison while everybody else's life has moved on. It's like dying mentally but still being physically present. So much depression, stress, people's hair falling out, so much stuff going on that it is impossible to describe it as a place you can go and enjoy yourself. I started recording and I got videos of the inside of the prison.

The day came for me to go. I experienced a lot, felt a lot, forgave other people, I was ready to go. When they came to my cell to tell me to pack up, I didn't run out or immediately pack up like I thought I would. I went to go talk to people that I got close to, prayed with them, shook their hand, and told them to keep their head up. I gave away a lot of stuff, my TV, commissary, shoes, hygiene products, and whatever I had to people that needed it.

The officer asked me, "Do you want to stay, or do you want to go?"

ant to be treated. The most important lesson I learned living for Christ is that He will remove people who don't belong in your life, and in most cases it's people you love and care about the most but it's for your own good. This new life is for the better, and for my good. This is my life, this is my heart, and Christ is my Lord and Savior. God bless you.

I was excited to leave but I wasn't in a rush. I knew that whatever was on the outside waiting for me would still be there. It took about two hours to get us checked out. When I walked out the gate, I thought I was going to cry, but my mentality was that I was going out to live and get everything God promised me. I got in the car and as I rode, I watched everything pass. We stopped at the store and there was a guy playing scratch off tickets. I heard him scream out like he lost again. I went over and gave him the bit of change I had left from buying food. When he asked me what it was for, I told him, "I just did ten years in prison, anything I can do to help somebody else, that's what I want to do." I gave him about six or seven dollars.

He said, "Man thank you man. God bless you man."

I got back in the car and went to go see my daughter. It was the first time I got to see my daughter in ten years. I hugged her but it was so awkward because we didn't know each other. I knew it was going to be a process and a journey to establish and develop a relationship with her. We walked around and spent time together before I went to go see my mom who I also hadn't seen in ten years. I was a little emotional when I saw my mom. She hugged me and told me I gained a lot of weight. I got to see my sister who kept in touch the entire time. She always wrote and called. They put me on Facebook live, and we went to sit on the porch to laugh, and hangout. It was in that moment where I thought, "I'm home, and I'm going to do everything God told me to do."

When I found Christ, I found peace from the chaos. When I found Christ, I found my identity. Giving my life to Christ opened my eyes to the lies that I was living and gave me the strength to overcome the person that life shaped me into. It gave me the ability to become who I am today. Giving my life to Christ helped me forgive and let go of offenses which allowed me to become a better father, son, brother, cousin, friend and man. Before Christ, I looked up to all the wrong examples thinking that was the way to live and that was the way to treat people. I treated people like pieces on a chessboard. Being in

the streets and living how I lived, you heartless and cold. I lived a life of par the streets you had to live on guard. I of everyone around me, even my friend has taught me to have a heart and comp people. I live without having to look ov shoulder or worrying about an early grav learned the results of a sinful lifestyle and of a righteous lifestyle. Living for Christ I that it's ok to trust again, and that I didn't with the mental torment, but I could have of mind that comes from Christ.

The Word of God taught me what r earth has taught me and that's love and how demonstrate it. When I understood love, I re the burden of hate that I lived with. Hate can anger and depression, but living for Christ has brought me joy. Living for Christ taught me to honest with myself and with other people. Lear who God called me to be and heeding His voic taught me how to provide for myself and my far Before Christ I didn't know how to love or how treat people, but I learned to treat others the way

I was excited to leave but I wasn't in a rush. I knew that whatever was on the outside waiting for me would still be there. It took about two hours to get us checked out. When I walked out the gate, I thought I was going to cry, but my mentality was that I was going out to live and get everything God promised me. I got in the car and as I rode, I watched everything pass. We stopped at the store and there was a guy playing scratch off tickets. I heard him scream out like he lost again. I went over and gave him the bit of change I had left from buying food. When he asked me what it was for, I told him, "I just did ten years in prison, anything I can do to help somebody else, that's what I want to do." I gave him about six or seven dollars.

He said, "Man thank you man. God bless you man."

I got back in the car and went to go see my daughter. It was the first time I got to see my daughter in ten years. I hugged her but it was so awkward because we didn't know each other. I knew it was going to be a process and a journey to establish and develop a relationship with her. We walked around and spent time together before I went to go see my mom who I also hadn't seen in ten years. I was a little emotional when I saw my mom. She hugged me and told me I gained a lot of weight. I got to see my sister who kept in touch the entire time. She always wrote and called. They put me on Facebook live, and we went to sit on the porch to laugh, and hangout. It was in that moment where I thought, "I'm home, and I'm going to do everything God told me to do."

When I found Christ, I found peace from the chaos. When I found Christ, I found my identity. Giving my life to Christ opened my eyes to the lies that I was living and gave me the strength to overcome the person that life shaped me into. It gave me the ability to become who I am today. Giving my life to Christ helped me forgive and let go of offenses which allowed me to become a better father, son, brother, cousin, friend and man. Before Christ, I looked up to all the wrong examples thinking that was the way to live and that was the way to treat people. I treated people like pieces on a chessboard. Being in the streets and living how I lived, you had to be heartless and cold. I lived a life of paranoia. Being in the streets you had to live on guard. I was suspicious of everyone around me, even my friends. Now Christ has taught me to have a heart and compassion for people. I live without having to look over my shoulder or worrying about an early grave or prison. I learned the results of a sinful lifestyle and the benefits of a righteous lifestyle. Living for Christ I've learned that it's ok to trust again, and that I didn't have to live with the mental torment, but I could have the peace of mind that comes from Christ.

The Word of God taught me what no man on earth has taught me and that's love and how to demonstrate it. When I understood love, I recognized the burden of hate that I lived with. Hate came with anger and depression, but living for Christ has brought me joy. Living for Christ taught me to be honest with myself and with other people. Learning who God called me to be and heeding His voice taught me how to provide for myself and my family. Before Christ I didn't know how to love or how to treat people, but I learned to treat others the way I want to be treated. The most important lesson I learned living for Christ is that He will remove people who don't belong in your life, and in most cases it's people you love and care about the most but it's for your own good. This new life is for the better, and for my good. This is my life, this is my heart, and Christ is my Lord and Savior. God bless you.